KidCaps' Presents

A Kids Guide to American wars - Volume 2:
World War I to The Korean War

KidCaps is An Imprint of BookCaps™

www.bookcaps.com

Table of Contents

About KidCaps

KidCaps is an imprint of BookCaps™ that is just for kids! Each month BookCaps will be releasing several books in this exciting imprint. Visit are website or like us on Facebook to see more!

Introduction

This book is a compilation of three different KidCaps books; it is the second of a three part series that presents American wars in a way that is easy to understand.

American soldiers fighting in World War One had to face all kinds of new weapons, including poison gas.[1]

---

[1] Image source: http://blais.wikispaces.com/World+War+One+(HAP)

World War I

Introduction

Harry was sweating because it was so hot. That was nothing new; in his military uniform Harry often felt hot, especially when he had to put on his gas mask. The mask covered up his entire face and sometimes he had to wear it for hours at a time. But even when he wasn't wearing his mask, his thick uniform- meant to protect him against the cold winter temperatures of Western France, made him feel hot all summer long.

Fighting in the war wasn't at all how he had expected it would be. He still remembered how his grandpa used to talk about the Civil War, fighting against the Confederates, and it all seemed so fascinating, as if it were a book or a movie. The soldiers seemed like heroes who never made mistakes and who always won the battle. His grandpa had a sparkle in his eye when he described rushing down hills of Gettysburg towards the enemy and rounding up "Johnny Rebs" as prisoners, as he had nicknamed them.

Harry had thought that fighting in the "Great War" as all the newspapers were calling it, would be something like that. He thought he would be running across fields and ducking under bullets, raising the American flag on a hilltop and basking in the glory of war. But he found that he hadn't been doing much of anything since arriving. He had been among the first Americans (or "Doughboys", as the French had called them) to arrive in Europe to fight against Germany and Austria-Hungary. After a few months of training and helping out the Allies in other ways, he had been moved to the Western front in October.

The front lines were actually trenches; miles and miles of trenches. Harry had helped to dig some of them himself. As he was digging, he could never have imagined that the next year of his life would be spent living underground like a mole. He slept, ate, stood guard, and even used the bathroom in the trenches. He stood up to fire his gun sometimes, but always from inside the safety trench. He had heard that the men used to rush out of the trenches to fight, but they didn't do that anymore. Not with those German machine guns so close by.

A hundred yards away, the Germans were in trenches of their own. Sometimes, when the nights were quiet, he could hear them talking and moving around, and could even see the light from their fires. In between the two trenches, there was an area of land, about a hundred yards wide, called "No Man's Land". No Man's Land was full of barbed wire, land mines, and the bodies of dead soldiers who had been shot trying to make it to the other side. Sometimes, the soldiers on each side would spend hours firing at each other and shooting shells to the other side. Harry heard that during some days like that thousands of men on each side would die, and yet neither army would move an inch. It seemed like a waste.

The shelling was the worst. Harry didn't dare stand up or leave the protection of his trench, but sometimes he felt like he was just sitting in a grave, waiting to die. Time moved so slowly when they were shooting those shells. He could hear them whistle by and sometimes they would explode to his right or to his left. So far, they hadn't gotten him, but Harry knew that his luck wouldn't last forever.

The Great War was not at all what Harry had expected. He had expected glorious battles and heroes and claiming hills and cities for the Allies. Instead, he spent hours waiting for the fighting to start, and then when it did start, he prayed that it would be over quickly. The Great War seemed to just keep dragging on and on. So many people were dying, but nothing seemed to change. Harry wondered how long the fighting would continue, how much longer he would have to walk around in his muddy trench and wait for something to happen.

When you think of World War One, also called the "Great War", what do you think of? It's easy to think of wars in the past as exciting times, but as you can imagine, there was also a lot of tragedy. Lots of people died, and it wasn't always the bad guys who were the ones dying. Sometimes, it wasn't easy even to know who the bad guys were. As you could see from the above description, World War One was a new type of war where different weapons were used, new tactics were tried out, and greater numbers of soldiers and governments participated than ever before. In this handbook, we will be getting a closer look at this amazing period of time.

First, we will look at what led up to what was called "the war to end all wars". How did so many countries end up fighting each other anyway, and what actually started the war? Then, we will find out more about how the United States came to be involved. We will see that although most Americans, including President Woodrow Wilson, did not want to fight in the war, the opinion of many began to change after several noteworthy things happened.

The next section will tell us what kinds of things actually happened during the war. We will find out what the American troops saw and experienced when they arrived in Europe and how they helped the Allied forces. We will find out about some of the new tactics and weapons used. For example, have you ever heard of mustard gas? Do you know what it is and why it is so dangerous?

Then, we will see what it was like to be a kid back then. Although kids weren't allowed to fight in the war, they were affected by it. Life in the United States changed a lot during the War, and kids genuinely saw the changes. The lessons they learned in school, their families, and even the food they ate was all affected by the war. Some of the changes were good, but some weren't so easy to deal with.
The section after that will tell us more about how World War One came to an end. Then, we will see what happened after. The war had long term effects, not just for Europe and the countries that fought, but for the entire world. In fact, we will see how some of the events that World War One caused directly led to World War Two and beyond.

As you read this handbook, try not to make the mistake of thinking that just because about one hundred years has passed that all of this is ancient history. Don't think that none of this matters to you or your life. Why shouldn't you think that? Well, we will see that World War One specifically shaped the world that we live in today. And we're not just talking about the governments; we are talking about families and even the way that people think. This Great War changed how the whole world sees war and other nations.

This handbook is going to teach you more about one of the most critical period of human history: it was a time a vast part of the human race was actively working to support this war, either fighting in it, helping the soldiers, of keeping the country running until the soldiers came home. Ask your parents if anyone in your family fought in World War One, and try to imagine what it was like for them as we look closer. Are you ready? Then let's begin!

Chapter 1: What led up to World War One?

Some pictures of the weapons and fighting from World War One.[2]

Have a look at the picture above. It looks pretty scary, right? There are ruins from buildings that have been destroyed, there are planes and tanks ready for battle, there are men wearing gas masks and firing machine guns, and there are destroyers and battleships fighting against submarines. World War One was a war when the most powerful nations in the world tried out new and dangerous weapons against each other. Before it was all over, some 70 million soldiers would be fighting all across Europe and the Atlantic Ocean, and about 10 million of them world be killed. Sadly, another 7 million civilians (people who weren't doing any of the fighting) would also die as a direct result of the war.

Of course, no one could know exactly what the final results of the war were going to be, but there was no doubt that with so many powerful nations involved, this war would be different than all other wars previously fought. But the question is: why did so many nations decided to fight each other at the same time? In other words, what caused World War One? As we will see, there were two main causes of the war, and one principal event. Let's find out more.

Cause number one: Imperialism. Do you what the word "imperialism" means? Imperialism is when one nation tries to become strong by establishing colonies all over the world and then demanding money and services from those colonies. For example, think about what happened with Great Britain and the United States. Great Britain sent a group of colonists to Jamestown, Virginia, in order to conquer the New World and to start making some money from it. More and more people were sent to help, and in time, the American colonists supplied food, cotton, workers, soldiers, and tax money to Great Britain. Great Britain used all it received from the colonies to become even stronger and to colonize even more areas of the world (like Africa and Asia). In that way, it became an Imperialist Power (also called an Empire). In fact, just before World War One broke out, people would say that the sun never set on the British Empire because it had colonies all over the world!

Great Britain was hardly the only country doing this. France, Portugal, Spain, Germany, and even the United States were all trying to find new areas of the world to colonize and from which they could receive economic and political benefits. Africa especially was carved up and divided like a turkey during Thanksgiving. Eventually, around the turn of the century, the large empires of the world found themselves in kind of an interesting position: there were no new areas that they could colonize. As a result, the thought came to be that the only way to get ahead and to grow stronger as a nation would be to take someone else's colony. In other words, for a country like Great Britain to get stronger, they would have to take colonies away from someone else, like France, Germany, or the United States.

Because so many countries wanted to be the strongest, many of them began to build bigger and better navies, armies, and to develop new weapons to give to their armies. Germany especially began to feel that it was their turn to become the dominant European power and to have the strongest navy, instead of Great Britain.

Seeing that some countries were starting to build up their armies and navies, and were working hard to develop new weapons and war technologies, a lot of people started to think a massive war in the near future was unavoidable. They were sure that, sooner or later, someone would try to steal the colonies that they had worked hard to get. To protect themselves, most of the imperialist countries began to form alliances with their neighbors in Europe. Do you know what an "alliance" is? Let's find out more, because the alliances made by the greatest powers were a second direct cause of World War One.

Cause number two: Alliances. We spoke about imperialism, and how because they wanted more colonies (and to protect their own interests) a lot of powerful nations began to make alliances with other countries. Do you know what an alliance is? An alliance is like a specific agreement that says "if there's a war, we won't attack you. If you need our help during a war, we will give it to you. In return, you promise not to attack us and to give us help if we need it." An alliance is a pretty fundamental thing during peacetime and during a war.

In Europe, Austria-Hungary made an alliance with Germany, and England, France, and Russia all made alliances with each other. Belgium had been declared a neutral state since the mid-1800s, so everyone knew that they wouldn't be a threat.

As a result of all this army-building and alliance-making, something fascinating happened just before the war broke out: everyone began to call Europe a "powder keg". A powder keg was a barrel used a long time ago to store black powder, a tremendously explosive material used in bullets and dynamite. What do you think would happen if you put a lit match or a candle too close to a powder keg? You can imagine the immense explosion that would result. Well, a lot of people started to look at the political situation in Europe and to call it a powder keg. Why do you think they did this?

Al of the countries wanted more power, so they built up their armies and navies and manufactured more and more guns and bombs. However, they began to worry about what their neighbors were up to, so they made secret alliances, promising to help each other out and get involved if there should be a war. Everyone had lots of weapons, had promised to fight if asked to, and was worried about protecting their own interests. As you can see, it wouldn't take much for a small war to start between two countries, and then for everyone else to get involved in that war because of the alliances.

As it turns out, that is exactly what happened. Once the conditions were perfect, all it took was one little match for the "powder keg of Europe" to explode into World War One. What was that powder keg? It was the assassination of Austro-Hungarian Archduke Franz Ferdinand, heir to the Austro-Hungarian throne. Let's learn more.

Principal event: The assassination of Archduke Franz Ferdinand. Everyone in Europe was waiting for a reason to start a war somewhere, and they finally got their reason on June 28, 1914, when Austria-Hungary declared war on Serbia. While these two countries had problems before this time, and had tried to make peace, things were different now. What had caused war between these two countries? It was the assassination of an important Austro-Hungarian political figure named Francis Ferdinand by a nationalist trained by the Serbian government on June 28, one month before. One month after the assassination, Austria-Hungary declared war on Serbia.

The assassination of Archduke Francis Ferdinand and his wife.[3]

Although the assassination was certainly a tragedy, no one could guess how quickly things would develop. By the end of August, Germany, Britain, France, Russia, and even Japan had all decided to honor their alliances and to fight on their respective sides of the war. No one thought that the war would be too serious, and, in fact, many thought that it would be over in one or two short months with a minimal loss of life.

Looking back, of course, we can see that things happened decidedly differently. World War One had begun, but the United States was still not involved. What made the Americans finally decided to join the fight? Let's find out.

---

[3] Image source: http://www.guardian.co.uk/world/2008/sep/25/firstworldwar.exhibition

Chapter 2: Why did Americans decide to fight in World War One?

So far, the Great War was all about things that happened in Europe. So why did the U.S. get involved? At first, the United States did not want to enter World War One to fight. Why not? Well, they felt that it was not their fight. Americans had no treaties with Austria-Hungary or with Serbia, and did not want to spend their money and sacrifice the lives of their soldiers fighting someone else's war. In fact, the United States initially wanted to be a kind of "peacemaker" between the two sides. President Woodrow Wilson, who had been elected in 1912, said that the United States should have strict neutrality in both word and deed.

For about two years, the United States stood back and watched the soldiers in Europe fight each other. They were horrified to hear about some of the terrible fighting going on, like during the first day of the Battle of the Somme. On July 1, 1916, the British army saw 57,470 men became casualties of war when fighting against the Germans. Of that huge number, 19,240 were killed or died of wounds. Another 8,000 Germans troops and 7,000 French troops died, for a total of about 34,000 troops dying on one day, roughly the same as what had happened during the entire battle of Gettysburg during the American Civil War.

However, although they were shocked, the American people, especially the farmers and the middle class, wanted nothing to do with the war. But as time went by, the upper class began to see its economic interests threatened by the war. Do you remember what we learned about imperialism, and how it was one of the causes of the Great War? Well, the United States even started to get a little worried about its economic and what would happen after the war. They were worried that the winners wouldn't take them into consideration and that they would lose their economic superiority in the future. As a result, a lot of businessmen and politicians began to urge the President and Congress to go to war. But not everyone was convinced yet. It was still Europe's war, and the United States didn't have a real reason to fight yet.

As time went by, a few things happened that started to change the opinion of the American people and to convince them that they should enter into the war and that they had a real reason to fight. Let's look at four of the events that influenced American opinion, and that eventually led them to join the fighting in Europe.

The "rape of Belgium": As you may remember, Belgium had tried to let the whole world know that they were neutral as far as wars went. They would not make alliances with anyone, but they also would not fight against anyone. All of Europe agreed to respect Belgium and to acknowledge that it was not a threat. But all that changed early in the war when Germany decided to invade Belgium in order to gain a military advantage against France. While marching through Belgium, the soldiers began to carry out acts of the worst kind, hurting a lot of people. Imagine that you were an American back then, reading about it in a newspaper.

Belgian civilians, including women and children, were killed in their houses, and then the houses were burnt to the ground over the dead bodies. Antique books, food supplies, factories- all were destroyed in order to prevent the Belgians from fighting back. The Germans were convinced that many Belgians were actually secret soldiers, so they felt justified in these actions. Over 20,000 buildings were eventually destroyed, 6,000 Belgians were killed, and another 1.5 million civilians ran away from their homes and towns to avoid the German army.

As you can imagine, news of these terrible actions shocked the world, but especially was the United States shocked. Called "the rape of Belgium" (to describe how awful the German soldiers had acted) the governments of the Allied forces soon began to tell everyone about what had happened to let them see that Germany and its armies needed to be stopped. Many Americans started paying attention, realizing that the war wasn't just about protecting their economic interests anymore, but to protect innocent civilians in Europe from suffering any other terrible things that the German army might do to them.

The sinking of the *Lusitania*: The *Lusitania* was a British cruise liner that went back and forth between the United States and Great Britain. Built in 1907, it was one of the world's largest ships, carrying both cargo and passengers across the Atlantic. After war broke out in 1914, the ship began to carry supplies for the British in order to help with the war effort. After leaving New York harbor on May 5, the ship was sunk by a German U-Boat (submarine) on May 7, 1915, killing all 1,198 aboard (including 128 Americans). It was a massive loss of life, but now Americans were among the dead by German hands.

The *HMS Lusitania* was sunk by a German submarine on May 7, 1915.[4]

The fact that a passenger ship, with American passengers, was sunk by a German submarine made the United States and its people furious. President Woodrow Wilson tried to keep the American people calm, saying that the country was "too proud" to be drawn into war over something like that. However, the American people started to view the German government and military differently as they had now personally been affected by the Great War.

Germany's unrestricted submarine warfare: By early 1917, Germany wanted to get the war over with and to get a quick victory. It was decided to have unrestricted submarine warfare, which is exactly what it sounds like. No restrictions. Anyone could be a target. Every boat not flying a German flag would be considered a target, even non-military and commercial ships. This action would be especially offensive to Americans, who had asked Germany to stop that exact same behavior back in 1916 after a French ship called the *Sussex* was torpedoed without warning.

During the agreement, Germany had promised to only target military ships, and that merchant ships could only be attacked after it had been verified that they had military supplies on board, and the crew had been safely transported off the ship.

---

[4] Image source: http://en.wikipedia.org/wiki/File:RMS_Lusitania_coming_into_port,_possibly_in_New_York,_1907-13-crop.jpg

But beginning in January 1917, the Germany government decided to again begin unrestricted submarine warfare against all kinds of targets. Five American merchant ships were sunk in March, and the American people now felt that they had been directly attacked by the German government and that the Germans needed to be punished and stopped.

The Zimmerman telegram: As if to let the American people know exactly how Germany saw them, the Foreign Secretary of the German Empire, Arthur Zimmermann sent a secret telegram to the German ambassador in Mexico on 16 January 1917. This telegram was intercepted by British agents and given to the United States on February 24. What did the secret telegram say?

Basically, the telegram was to try to get the Mexican government's help in fighting against the U.S. With its renewed efforts at carrying out unrestricted submarine warfare, Germany knew that the United States would get seriously upset and probably enter the war (they were right) and so they wanted the Mexican government to keep the U.S. busy fighting a war at home. In return, the Germans promised money, ammunition, and the return of Mexican lands given up to the U.S. during the Mexican American War, specifically Texas, New Mexico, and Arizona.

When the American people saw what the Zimmerman telegram said (and Zimmerman himself later confirmed it during an interview) it was so shocking and revealed what the Germans were willing to do in order to win. Although Mexico never took the offer seriously, the American people were tremendously upset and demanded action. They didn't just want to help others fight or to prepare for war anymore; they wanted to fight it themselves! They realized that the Germany government wanted to war against the American people. If a war was what they wanted, a war is what they would get!

As a result, on April 2, 1917, President Woodrow Wilson went before the United States Congress to ask for permission to declare war against Germany. On April 6, Congress voted and approved the request. You can read the text of the resolution below:

> "Joint Resolution Passed by the United States Senate and House of Representatives Effective April 6, 1917, at 1:18 p.m.
>
> WHEREAS, The Imperial German Government has committed repeated acts of war against the Government and the people of the United States of America; therefore, be it
> Resolved, by the Senate and House of Representatives of the United States of America in Congress assembled, That the state of war between the United States and the Imperial German Government, which has thus been thrust upon the United States, is hereby formally declared; and That the President be, and he is hereby, authorized and directed to employ the entire naval and military forces of the United States and the resources of the Government to carry on war against the Imperial German Government; and to bring the conflict to a successful termination all the resources of the country are hereby pledged by the Congress of the United States."[5]

---

[5] Quotation source: http://www.nationalcenter.org/DeclarationofWWI.html

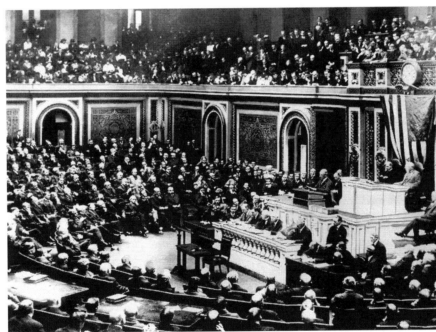

President Wilson asks Congress for permission to declare war on Germany.[6]

The United States had officially entered World War One!

[6] Image source: http://www.businessinsider.com/pimco-the-us-will-get-downgraded-2012-10

Chapter 3: What did the United States do during World War One?

After officially declaring war against Germany, the United States spent the first few months preparing for the war that it would be fighting in. This included starting a draft to increase the size of the armies, increasing production of war materials in factories, and the training of military personnel. In all, some 4 million Americans would be mobilized as part of the military, and every home across the country would be affected in one way or another.

In June of 1917, the first American troops arrived in France to help with the war against Germany. The Europeans soldiers called the Americans "doughboys". Why? The nickname was exceedingly old, back from the days of the Mexican-American War. Observers from Europe saw the U.S. infantry marching across the hot, dusty Texan desert and thought that the soldiers, covered from head to toe in dust, looked like bakers covered in flour while making dough. Because of that, American infantrymen were called doughboys up until World War Two, when they began to be called G.I. Joes. Despite the nickname, the French and British were happy to see the American troops arrive.

The initial plan was for the Americans to focus of supporting the French and British troops fighting on the "Western Front" of the war. However, as time went by, American troops also ended up fighting in Russia, on the eastern front, and in Italy. By the spring of 1918, some 10,000 American troops were arriving daily.

The first substantial contribution of American troops (called the American Expeditionary Forces) was helping to repel what came to be called the Spring Offensive. When the Germans resumed unrestricted submarine warfare in the Atlantic, they knew that the Americans would be forced to enter the war. However, they thought that the Americans while strong economically, were not unusually strong when it came to military and supplies. They thought that, by the time, the Americans were ready to fight the war would be over already.

They were decidedly wrong.

The Americans arrived on the Western front just when the Allies most needed them. The Allies had been fighting for years and were tired, so fresh troops and more weapons helped to change the situation on their favor. The Spring Offensive of 1918 was a series of four strong attacks by the Germans. The Germans were able to move forward quite a bit against the Allied forces and gain some territory. By the end of the first day, over 20,000 British had died and another 35,000 were wounded.

A tank full of German soldiers on the first day of the Spring Offensive, March 21, 1918.[7]

However, the attacks were not very well organized, and the troops quickly ran out of food and supplies as they marched. The Allies (with the Americans fighting them) were able to keep the Germans from winning any significant targets.

The Allies struck back on August 8, beginning what came to be called the Hundred Days Offensive. By September, the Germans were forced back to where they had started from. By November, the German army had been pushed back so far that they had to consider surrendering. The large number of American troops helped the Allies to fight back against the Germans.

But what was it actually like for the Americans who were fighting. It would be one thing to look at a map and to talk about this battle or that battle, but it would be an entirely different thing to discuss being in the battles themselves, smelling the smells and seeing the sights. Let's go back for a moment and pretend that we are fighting alongside the Allied forces during the Hundred Day Offensive. What would we have seen and experienced?

First, we would have experienced the actual boat ride over to Europe. In those days, troops were moved by ship across the Atlantic to where the fighting was. But what do you remember about the Atlantic Ocean? What was happening there? That's right! There were German submarines, called U-Boats, which were sinking all kinds of ships that were suspected of being used by the Allies. The Germans thought that they had the perfect plan because it was devilishly hard to sink a U-Boat.

However, the Allies came up with a way of avoiding the U-Boats: they travelled in convoys, or groups of ships. So imagine that you are a soldier travelling across the Atlantic. Instead of just being on one ship in the middle of the ocean, all by yourself, you are now part of a group of about ten or fifteen ships. Two or three are like yours- loaded with soldiers and materials- while the rest are destroyers and battleships that are there to protect you. They have guns and torpedoes to fight against the submarines. Would you have felt safer? As it was, most of the Americans soldiers going to Europe made it there without any problems.

---

[7] Image source: http://en.wikipedia.org/wiki/File:Bundesarchiv_Bild_183-P1013-316,_Westfront,_deutscher_Panzer_in_Roye.jpg

Once you arrived in Europe, you would start to see that the war was not at all like you had imagined it. Like Harry, from the introduction, you would have seen that the war wasn't about glorious charges and heroes running up hills' it was months and months of men sitting in trenched and shooting guns and bombs at each other. Can you imagine how slowly the time passed? The men who were there said that what they remember the most was the mud and the smell of dead soldiers everywhere.

During World War One, American troops saw things that no other soldiers had ever seen before. They saw chemical weapon used to hurt and kills thousands of people at a time. Weapons like Mustard Gas (named because of its smell) would make people's skin and lungs burn, making it difficult for them to fight if it didn't kill them. Machine guns would kill entire groups of men at a time. Instead of the Revolutionary War and the Civil War where men were killed one at a time by guns that needed to be reloaded, both the German and the Allied armies could kills dozens of men in a matter of seconds.

In the "no man's land" between the trenches, barbed wire slowed down armies when they tried to march, and hidden land mines would explode and destroy their legs and feet. Shells (missiles shot from cannons) could be shot from behind the trenches into the enemies trenches. The soldiers who lived through the war say that they felt the most afraid during the shelling. There was no escape. All they could do was sit and wait for it to stop, hoping that the next bomb didn't fall on them.

It was a terrifying war, and one that was so different than all other previous wars. The American soldiers fought for months with the Allies, but sometimes there would be little to show for their efforts. They would be in the same trenches shooting at the same people as before. It wasn't until the Hundred Day Offensive that things seriously started to change.

Chapter 4: What was it like to be a kid during World War One?

While kids didn't do any of the fighting in World War One (that was left to the adults), they were directly affected by the Great War. After all, think of all of the families that were left alone when the fathers and older brothers left to fight in the war. And did you know something sad? 110,000 Americans died as a direct result of World War One. About half died during the actual fighting, and the other half died soon afterwards because of a terrible disease that spread called the Spanish Influenza. Now imagine how many families were left without a dad or without a brother.

Death is part of the reality of war, and it is not glorious at all. War is much different than the books and the movies like to make it. It hurts, it's scary, and everybody just wants it to end. Sometimes war has to happen to stop majorly bad people from doing extremely bad things, but World War One taught everyone that armed conflict should be avoided wherever possible.

Kids on both sides of the Atlantic Ocean were affected because of the war. For instance, in the United States, kids saw the world around them change almost overnight. The lessons that they learned in school were changed to include more material in support of the war and against the enemy. Food was harder to get so many families began to grow what were called "victory gardens". It was believed that each American could contribute to the war effort by giving more to the troops fighting and living simpler lives back home.

Kids who were part of clubs began to try to sell war bonds. Do you know what a war bond was? It was when people would buy a certificate from the government. It was like loaning money to the government to help with the war. Then, when the war was over, the people could get their money back by trading in the certificate. Boy Scouts went door to door to try to sell war bonds to their neighbors.

Women went to go work in the factories to make weapons and other materials for the soldiers fighting in the war. For kids, this was a monumental change. Instead of always having their mothers at home, cooking and cleaning, now the house was empty during the day. As for the women, they saw that they could have a pivotal role in the community and in the country as a whole. Many women enjoyed working outside of the house and, even after the war ended, they stayed at their jobs.

When younger kids grew up, many of them would be drafted to fight in World War I and later in World War II.

In Europe, the kids living there were affected by the war too. Do you remember how tens of thousands of soldiers died on both sides? Think of all the British, the French, and even the German kids who lost their dads and brothers during the fighting. Think about how many of them had to run away from their houses to avoid being hurt by the enemy soldiers. Some entire towns were destroyed. Can you imagine all the buildings in your entire town, including your school, your church, and your house, being destroyed by strange men who want to hurt you? Some of those kids grew up with some seriously unpleasant memories of things they saw and experienced.

After the war happened, the economy of Germany got particularly bad, and the money started to suffer from inflation. Do you know what inflation is? Inflation is where the value of money goes down, and the prices go way way up. People might pay thousands of dollars for a loaf of bread! In fact, money got to be so worthless that kids would play with packets of money as if they were blocks! Look at the picture below!

German kids played with worthless money as if it were blocks.[8]

As you can imagine, some kids living in Europe started to wonder if they would have enough food for the following day. That would be pretty scary, don't you think?

Kids, even though they didn't do any of the fighting, were still hugely affected by what happened during World War One.

---

[8] Image source: http://www.thehistoryblog.com/archives/7742

Chapter 5: How did World War One end?

When the American troops arrived in the spring of 1918, the victory that the German thought they had was no longer so sure. The Allies were not only able to hold off their attack during their Spring Offensive, but they were able to push back and win battle after battle during the Hundred Day Offensive. The Americans helped the allies to push the Germans back past the trenches they had dug and into their own territory. Eventually, their battle lines collapsed, and German high command accepted that they had lost the war. An armistice, or cease fire, was signed on November 11, 1918, ending the war.

In Versailles, France, a formal treaty was signed on June 28, 1919, exactly five years after the assassination of Archduke Francis Ferdinand that had started the war. The treaty officially established peace between the different countries, but it also punished Germany for its actions during the war. How so? In addition to claiming responsibility for the war, (together with Austria-Hungary) Germany would have to disarm and pay heavy fines (called reparations) to some of the enemy countries to help fix the damage from the war. These fines were so heavy that they seriously hurt the German economy, something which led to other unexpected event in the future as we shall see.

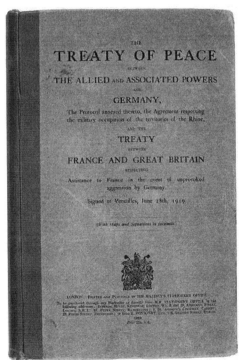

The Treaty of Versailles was singed on June 28, 1919.[9]

The United States helped to negotiate the treaty, and part I included the formation of something called the League of Nations (we will learn more in a moment). Congress could never agree 100% on whether or not the treaty was good for American interests, so in 1921 the treaty was rejected, and a specific agreement called the Knox–Porter Resolution brought an official end to the war between the United States and the other nations (although they hadn't been really fighting for almost two years).

[9] Image source: http://en.wikipedia.org/wiki/File:Treaty_of_Versailles,_English_version.jpg

After lots of negotiations, the world finally had peace again. The Great War, the War to End All Wars, had ended.

Chapter 6: What happened after World War One?

The League of Nations that had been created by the Treaty of Paris was supposed to be a special organization. Its headquarters was to be in Geneva, Switzerland, and it would be a place where representatives from all countries could get together and talk openly about international problems and disputes. The purpose of the organization was simple: prevent another world war from happening.

Each country would be able to discuss border problems, political problems, oppression, and even economic problems with other nations. They could ask for and receive help, and nations that acted poorly would suffer penalties and consequences. The League of Nations, promoted heavily by Woodrow Wilson, looked like it just might bring a new era of peace to the world and help it to avoid serious conflicts in the future. Unfortunately, as history shows, another world war did come about twenty years after the first one ended. And, yet again, Germany was the principal aggressor. What had happened during those twenty years and why couldn't the League of Nations prevent it?

The League of Nations had focused on disarmament, on trying to get the key countries to give up their weapons. However, neither the Treaty of Paris nor the League of Nations itself was hugely successful in getting Germany to get rid of its weapons. As Germany kept getting stronger, other nations were too scared to give up their weapons because they thought that Germany might attack them and they wanted to be able to defend themselves and their families.

Germany itself had been hurt by the Treaty of Versailles and by all of the reparations that they had to pay. However, the German people got so desperate for the good old days that they elected a man named Adolf Hitler (who had fought in World War I) to the position of Chancellor and believed his promises that he could make Germany strong like it had been before. The people were tired of being poor and they felt taken advantage of by the other nations. As a result, many of them stood by, and others even supported Hitler as he started the next world war. The League of Nations was eventually disbanded because it failed to meet its goal (although it would be reinvented later as the United Nations).

After the war, Russia also saw some substantial changes. For some time before the Great War, the people had not been happy with their rulers. During World War I, the Russian army suffered many defeats on the Eastern front at the hands of the German army. Even though the leader Tsar Nicholas II took personal control of the army, the situation on the battlefield got worse and worse. At home, the people suffered from lack of food and political problems. In February of 1917, a large scale revolution out the power in the hands of the people, and a second revolution in October put it in the hands of the Communist Party, leading to the formation of the Soviet Union in 1922. World War I was a direct trigger leading to the formation of the U.S.S.R. and, by extension, the Cold War and proxy wars (where the US and USSR used other countries to fight their war, like in Vietnam) that followed later.

Another significant change was seen in the culture of the United States itself. Do you remember how the role of women had changed during the war? Instead of staying at home, they were working in the factories and earning money for their kids. Some of the men did not come back; so many women had to keep working in order to pay the bills. As a result of their increased activities on behalf of the community, many women demanded the right to vote, and it was given to them on August 18, 1920.

There were single-parent families and families who had to deal with death. The entire culture of the American people, instead of being optimistic about the future, became doubtful and cynical. They began to look differently even at their neighbors. During the war, Americans were worried that spies were everywhere. After the war, it was hard to stop looking at their neighbors with suspicion.

The world had changed as a direct result of World War One. People weren't as trusting; they were more focused on work, and they realized how easily everything that they love could be torn away from them. Moreover, the stage had already been set for the next "War to End All Wars", World War Two and the Cold War that would follow.

Conclusion

We have learned a lot about World War One, especially about what the United States did during it and its effects afterwards. Would you have liked to have been alive back then? Probably not. After all, it was such a difficult time and such awful things happened. If you had been a soldier, you would have seen death and destruction every day. If you had been a kid, you would have been worried about your family members fighting, about losing your house, or about where your next meal would come from. Let's take a moment to review all that we learned in this handbook.

First, we looked at what led up to what was called "the war to end all wars". Do you remember: how did so many countries end up fighting each other anyway, and what actually started the war? We learned about imperialism, and how it made so many countries worry about what might happen to their economic power if a war were to happen. We saw that all sorts of alliances were made and weapons were stored up, making Europe into a "powder keg". Finally, a match came and made the powder keg explode- the assassination of Archduke Francis Ferdinand in June of 1914. One by one, all of the nations honored their treaties and went to war.

Then, we found out more about how the United States came to be involved. Although most Americans, including President Woodrow Wilson, did not want to fight in the war, the opinion of many began to change after several noteworthy things happened. Among these momentous events was the "Rape of Belgium" where the whole world heard about the terrible things done by the German army to the people of Belgium. The, the unrestricted submarine warfare and the Zimmerman telegram were the final events that made Americans agree to go help the Allies to defeat Germany.

The next section told us what kinds of things actually happened during the war. We found out what the American troops saw and experienced when they arrived in Europe and how they helped the Allied forces. We learned about trench warfare and how scary it was to just sit and wait sometimes while the enemy was shooting shells. We found out about some of the new tactics and weapons used. For example, we learned about mustard gas and how dangerous it was to soldiers, and we saw how deadly machine guns were to both sides.

Then, we saw what it was like to be a kid back then. Although kids weren't allowed to fight in the war, they were affected by it. Life in the United States changed a lot during the War, and kids actually saw the changes. The lessons they learned in school, their families, and even the food they ate was all affected by the war. Some of the changes were good, but some weren't so easy to deal with.

The section after that told us more about how World War One came to an end. We saw how the American soldiers helped the Allies to push back against the Germans and to participate in the Hundred Days Offensive, which ended with the German surrender and an armistice (a cease fire). Finally, the Treaty of Versailles was signed in June of 1919.

Finally, we saw what happened after the war had finished. The war had long term effects, not just for Europe and the countries that fought, but for the entire world. For example, the reparations that Germany was forced to pay led to extreme inflation and to an economic depression. The whole country suffered so much and wanted things to get better so badly that they elected an extreme man, Adolf Hitler, to run their country. Eventually, this man was responsible for starting another world war. We also saw the formation of the League of Nations, an organization meant to help solve the world's problems. Although it failed, it gave people hope that maybe serious problems could be avoided, and so the United

Nations was formed. We also saw how World War One was a direct cause of the Russian revolution that led to the formation of the Soviet Union and the Cold War.

When we look at history, it's easy to think that what we are reading about has nothing to do with us. However, the things that happened yesterday shaped the world that we live in today. The wars that were fought created the laws, countries, and ideas that we learn in school and live by every day. World War One is a reminder of how terrible war can be, but it also explains the world around us.

World War II

American troops landed on Normandy Beach in France on Tuesday, June 6, 1944.[10]

---

[10] Image source: http://en.wikipedia.org/wiki/File:Into_the_Jaws_of_Death_23-0455M_edit.jpg

Introduction

Robert Jones was terrified. He felt all sorts of strange feelings moving through his brain and rippling across his body. He felt seasick as the little boat bounced up and down over the waves, moving ever closer to the beach and to all the smoke. His hands gripped his rifle and were numb from a combination of the chill of the early morning air and the cold metal. His stomach tightened in knots as he thought about what was about to happen to him and to the soldiers around him. His platoon of about 30 soldiers was part of the United States' Army First Infantry Division, 16th Infantry Regiment, and their little amphibious troop carrier had just been launched out of a landing ship towards Omaha Beach, near the city of Normandy, in France.

Robert looked at the men around him and saw that most of them looked like they felt the way he did. Although Robert was the only one from the town of Topeka, most of the men in his platoon were from his home state of Kansas. None of them were used to travelling on the water, especially not on the way to fight in a war. One man threw up on the floor of the little boat, but no one said anything or made fun of him. They were all scared. The high walls of the boat didn't let them see what was going on around them, and they weren't too sure how much longer they had to wait. There were four men operating the boat, and those guys were too busy avoiding the obstacles put up by the German Army to talk to the soldiers.

Robert had heard the planes flying overhead during the night and knew that they were supposed to be bombing the beachhead before he and the other soldiers arrived. He had also heard about some sort of a plan by the men in charge to fool the Germans into thinking that the attack would be in a different part of France. But Robert was just a private in the army, so he didn't actually know how any of those plans were going, and he certainly didn't have the right to ask anyone about them. All he could hope for was that there would be fewer bullets flying at him when he got off of the landing craft and onto the beach.

The pilot of the landing craft, who was called the coxswain, yelled out some orders to the other crew members. Robert and the rest of the soldiers couldn't hear exactly what they said, but they soon understood the meaning as they felt the boat stop moving forward towards the shoreline.

They had arrived at Omaha Beach.

The gigantic metal ramp at the front of the landing craft was lowered down by one of the crewman, and the soldiers went charging out into the shallow water near the beach. They were met with a scene of utter chaos. The man right in front of Robert, Harry Jenkins, from Auburn, was shot through the head before they even made it off the boat. Robert didn't have time to think about it or to be sad because the Platoon Leader was yelling at all of the men to run out onto the beach and to try to find some cover. Robert put his head down and ran forward with the rest of his platoon.

His boots sunk into the wet sand and the sand and water seemed to explode all around him. He was too scared to lift up his head to look around because he knew that his helmet was the only thing protecting him. All Robert could think about was getting to the pile of rocks that he saw in front of him. As he ran forward, he tripped on a dead body lying on the beach- it was his Platoon Leader, Jeff Baker, from Colorado. Robert ran forward and dove onto the ground, hiding behind the rocks.

To his right and to his left, he could see that about 25 men from his platoon had made it. In the shallow water and on the sand, he could count six dead bodies. The water was already turning red with the blood.

Further down the beach, he saw dozens of landing crafts like that one he had come in on lowering their ramps, and wave after wave of soldiers came spilling out onto the beach. His craft had already pulled itself back into the water and was heading back to the supply ship, the USS *Samuel Chase*, to bring more men to the beach.

His Platoon Sergeant had taken command of the group. Robert heard his name being yelled, and he snapped to attention. "Yes sir!" he yelled. The Sergeant explained that they were to take out the machine guns on the hill above them; otherwise no new troops would be able to make it to the beach. It would be difficult, and they would have to be smart, but the Sergeant knew that his men were up to the challenge. He asked the platoon if anyone had any grenades, and Robert showed the three that were clipped to his belt.

The Sergeant asked him: "Robert, how's your arm?"

With a nerv   "Sir, I once pitched
a no-hitter in

The Sergean   ose guns to make
them stop sh   to the base of that
hill?"

Robert lifted   st immediately a
hail of bullet   Yes, sir."

The Sergean   n rushed out
towards the   World War Two.
He was amo   more.

Over 160,000 soldiers, including 73,000 Americans, landed in Normandy on June 6, 1944.[11]

Can you imagine riding in the landing craft next to Robert and the other soldiers? Can you imagine storming out onto Omaha Beach to fight against the German Nazis? Can you imagine how scary and difficult it would have been? The men and women who fought in World War Two had to experience some terrible and terrifying things. They saw their friends die, they went to foreign lands to fight against awful enemies, and each morning when they woke up, they never knew if that would be their last day alive.

World War Two was finally won by the Allied forces, and Americans were proud fight alongside the Allies. But what was World War Two all about, and how did Americans get involved in it? This handbook is going to teach us all about this war and the role that Americans helped play in it.

First, we will look at what led up to the outbreak of World War Two. For example, do you know what event marked the start of the War, and what conditions made it possible? Do you know why the United States waited so long to get involved? We will find out in this section.

Then, we will learn about the event that made the United State formally enter the War and what some of the first things that they did were. After that, we will see how the United States fought in World War Two on two separate fronts: in the European Theater and in the Pacific Theater. We will see some of the challenges that American soldiers had to deal with and some of the things that they saw and experience. World War Two also saw new types of technology being used and new strategies employed on the battlefield.

The next section will talk about what it was like to be a kid back then. Although no kids were allowed to fight in World War Two on either side, they were affected by what was going on. Things at home changed, and even school and meals were affected. We will see what it was like to be a kid both in America and in Europe.

The following section will talk about something more positive: the end of World War Two. We will see what events finally led to the end of this global conflict, both in Europe and then in the Pacific. Finally, we will see what happened after the war ended, including both the short-term and long-term consequences of the war.

War is a terrible thing, of that we can be sure. People die, it is scary, and lots of damage is done to innocent people and cities. Families are broken up, and entire nations disappear from the map. Yet, as awful as war is, sometimes it is necessary. As we will see, the world was facing several threats by leaders who wanted to hurt others and to take over entire continents. They would not take no for an answer, and one of them even went so far as to try to kill an entire race of people. Men like that have to be stopped, and sometimes war is the only way to do it.

But why should you care about a war that happened over 70 years ago? While many of the people who lived during that war and who fought in it have since died, we are still living in the world that World War Two helped to create. And sometimes, there are lots of scary men out there who need to be stopped, so war continues to be a reality. While we hope to never see anything like World War Two ever again, there are lots of valuable lessons that we can learn.

---

[11] Image source: http://www.army.mil/d-day/slideshow.html

Are you ready to learn more about this important period of world history? Then let's begin with the first section.

Chapter 1: What Led Up to World War Two?

When you think of the causes of World War Two, you probably think of one person:

Adolf Hitler was the Chancellor of Germany during World War Two.[12]

While it is true that Adolf Hitler was one of the main aggressors during the war, he certainly could never have done all that he did were it not for certain political and economic conditions that existed at the time, and were it not for the similar political goals of Japan and Italy. The causes of World War Two are a little complex, but's let's take a minute to look at them, because then we will understand why so many people were willing to fight and die in this conflict.

Let's first look at what happened in Europe, shortly after World War One concluded. Do you remember who the principal aggressor was in that war? That's right: it was Germany! Germany had teamed up with Austria-Hungary to conquer all of Europe, including the neutral countries like Belgium. At the end of the war, after Germany had been forced to retreat after losing several pivotal battles, the Treaty of Versailles was signed to put an official end to the hostilities. Along with making peace, the Treaty of Versailles made Germany suffer a lot of consequences for having done so much damage during the war. Among other things, Germany agreed to pay "reparations" to the Allied powers in the equivalent of about US$442 billion today. But where did all of that money come from? The money had to come from the German economy, of course.

The Treaty of Versailles made it clear that the payments had to be made in gold or foreign currency-considered much more stable by the other countries. So in order to pay the debts, Germany had to convert its money into foreign currency in order to buy gold in order to pay the reparations. Got it? But as they kept buying more and more foreign currency and foreign gold, the value of the German currency went down, meaning that they needed more money to buy even basic items, like loaves of bread and bottles of milk. Soon, even basic items were almost impossible for the Germany people to obtain.

The difficult economic situation was bad enough, but there was also the German pride. In the Treaty of Versailles, note Article 231:

> "The Allied and Associated Governments affirm and Germany accepts the responsibility of Germany and her allies for causing all the loss and damage to which the Allied and Associated Governments and their nationals have been subjected as a consequence of the war imposed upon them by the aggression of Germany and her allies."

12 Image source: http://en.wikipedia.org/wiki/File:Bundesarchiv_Bild_183-S33882,_Adolf_Hitler_retouched.jpg

This article makes it clear that Germany (along with its allies) caused all the problems from World War One. Many of the German people felt insulted by this and thought that the whole world was laughing at Germany. This led to a feeling called "nationalism", where the people wanted to see their country receive the respect and attention that they thought it deserved. It was during this time; a time when the people were looking for a new type of government to fix the economic problems and to make Germany glorious again, that Adolf Hitler and his National Socialist political party came to power and Hitler started to carry out his dark plans for the country.

In the meantime, Italy had political ambitions of its own. Once home to the impressive and powerful Roman Empire, the country had since begun to experience economic problems and was no longer dominating the Mediterranean Sea as it once did. As Germany began to shift towards nationalistic goals (meaning goals that made people feel good about Germany) Italy saw a chance to take advantage of their strength and to make a formal agreement with them and announced it on November 1, 1936. This agreement would also help both sides to fight together against a new threat in Europe: Communism from Russia. Also, Italy hoped to once again become a powerful nation and to rule over the Mediterranean like before.

In the meantime, Japan had ambitions of its own. Because it desired to be the dominant country in Asia, it had begun to fight against China and even to invade Chinese lands and to kill innocent civilians. By 1937, the Empire of Japan and the Republic of China were already at war, and Japan was interested in finding someone to help them win their war, and to stop anyone who got in their way.

On September 27, 1940, Germany, Italy, and Japan signed a momentous agreement called the Tripartite Pact, and these three nations became known as the Axis alliance. Although they never got quite organized to be able to send money and troops to help each other out, they were united by their common goals of expanding their territories. The way they saw it, these three countries were going to be the dominant powers in Europe and Asia. Also, they all agreed that they hated Russian Communism and would do anything to stop it.

So the economic circumstances and political ambitions of these three countries were the principal reason for the outbreak of World War Two. When these countries decided to start attacking and mistreating their neighbors, the other countries of the world saw that the aggressors had to be stopped. Most historians feel that the official start to World War Two was on September 1, 1939, when Hitler's German Army invaded its innocent neighbor, Poland.

You may be asking yourself: where was the United States during all of this? Do you remember how the United States had fought in World War One? A lot of the people who were alive just twenty years later, when Hitler invaded Germany, had unusually unpleasant memories of fighting in Europe. They remembered how badly America had suffered along with the rest of the world and how so many American soldiers had died. Also, the country had just experienced a rough economic time called the Great Depression, so a lot of people were worried about making a terrible situation even worse.

In order to make sure that the United States didn't get involved in any more wars, Congress passed a series of laws called the Neutrality Acts. Three acts, passed between 1935 and 1937, made it impossible for the United States to trade weapons of supplies with nations who were at war (whether they were the good guys or the bad guys) and even prevented passengers from travelling on ships of nations at war. The goal was to keep the American people as far away as possible from the conflicts of other nations.

President Franklin D. Roosevelt, President of the U.S. at the time, had even said: "I have said this before, but I shall say it again and again: your boys are not going to be sent into any foreign wars."[13]

What do you think? Was that the best way for the American people to handle the situation? What would you have done if you had been the president?

Although he didn't want to get involved in other people's fights, President Roosevelt was still worried that the acts might end up helping the bad guys, like Germany. How so? If the U.S. were to stand by and not help England and France, then it could be like making the war easier for Germany, something that everyone agreed was a lousy idea. Finally, after Germany attacked Poland in 1939, the previous Neutrality Acts were repealed, and the United States was allowed to help out the Allied forces on a limited basis. In March of 1941, a new Act, called the Lend-Lease Act, ended American neutrality and allowed the U.S. to sell, lend, or even give weapons and other support to any nation that the government wanted to, even if that nation was at war.

Most Americans, including those in the government, had wanted to remain neutral. What changed their opinion? As was the case with World War One, the Americans began to hear about the terrible things happening in Europe, and they realized that a Europe dominated by extremists like Hitler and Mussolini (the dictator in Italy) would be ruinous for everyone.

United States ships began to escort other ships that were carrying supplies for the Allies, and some of these ships were sunk by German U-Boats (submarines) something that made many Americans angry and helped them to realize that the war was getting closer and closer to home.

The American people began to prepare for war, especially after France was defeated in 1940 and Italy allied itself with Germany. People began to ration food in order to give more supplies to the growing army. A peacetime draft was put into effect, the first in the nation's history, forcing American men to join the armed forces, although there were already lots of volunteers. Also, for the first time ever, women were allowed to play a larger role in the military. Some 110,000 women joined the Women's Army Auxiliary Corps (WAAC) and served both in the U.S. and overseas, in non-combat positions, allowing more men to go to the front and fight. Also, women began to serve in non-combat position in the Air Force, in an organization called the Women Air force Service Pilots (WASP), whose job was to help train anti-aircraft gunners by towing targets and to carry cargo from one place to another.

The United States was no longer neutral and was preparing for a fight that everyone knew was coming. However, they were still determined not to enter the fight unless they were forced to. What kind of an event could force the American people to support entry into World War Two- the most destructive of all wars in history? Let's find out.

---

[13] Quotation source: http://www.history.co.uk/explore-history/ww2/us-entry-and-alliance.html

Chapter 2: Why did the United States enter into World War Two?

As we have seen, the United States did not want to get involved in another country's war. But the American people as a whole would be willing to fight in a war if it meant protecting themselves and their interests. On December 7, 1941, the war that was raging around the world was brought to the American doorstep. What happened?

The Japanese had already made it clear that they wanted to dominate the continent of Asia and that they didn't want any interference by the United States or other Allied countries. In order to make sure that the U.S. and other countries would be unable to stop them, the Japanese Navy launched a preemptive strike on several different targets, including Pearl Harbor, in Hawaii. A "preemptive" strike is an attack that comes as a surprise, with no warning. Below, you can see a picture taken by a Japanese plane of that attack:

A torpedo causes an explosion on the *USS Oklahoma*.[14]

The goal was to destroy as much of the U.S. Navy in the Pacific as possible so that it would not be able to stop the nation of Japan from conquering Asia. Several other attacks in Thailand and Hong Kong, carried out at almost the same moment, also were aimed at stopping the Americans and other Allied countries from being able to fight back.

The attack at Pearl Harbor was truly devastating. Because the attack was totally unexpected, and because it came very early in the morning, many of the men were still sleeping and were not ready to fight. The planes were out in the open (to guard against sabotage) but that made them easy targets for the attackers. The Japanese planes came in two waves, dropping heavy bombs, torpedoes, and shooting machine gun fire. Submarines also took part, and historians think that one "midget" submarine (a small

[14] Image source: http://en.wikipedia.org/wiki/File:Attack_on_Pearl_Harbor_Japanese_planes_view.jpg

submarine launched by a larger boat that only carried two crew members) was able to sink the *USS Virginia*.

In total, the attack against Pearl Harbor and some local airfields lasted about ninety minutes, but the damage was particularly extensive. All eight U.S. Navy battleships that were stationed at Pearl Harbor were damaged, and four of them were sunk. Later, two of them were raised, and the other four were repaired so that eventually six of the eight went out to battle in the war. The Japanese planes also sank or damaged other smaller ships: three cruisers, three destroyers, an anti-aircraft training ship, and one minelayer. There were also other damages: 188 U.S. aircraft were destroyed during the attack, 2,402 Americans were killed and another 1,282 were wounded.

The *USS Arizona* was sunk after it was hit by a Japanese bomb.[15]

The attack was devastating, and the American people realized that they could no longer be neutral in the war. They realized that the war was about defending themselves as well as stopping the bad guys who wanted to hurt others. The next day, on December 8, 1941, President Roosevelt went before Congress and delivered a speech in which he spoke about how awful it was what the Japanese had done, and how the American people had to react. He outlined how dangerous the nation of Japan was acting and in his speech he said:

> "Yesterday, December 7th, 1941 -- a date which will live in infamy -- the United States of America was suddenly and deliberately attacked by naval and air forces of the Empire of Japan... The attack yesterday on the Hawaiian Islands has caused severe damage to American naval and military forces. I regret to tell you that very many American lives have been lost. In

15 Image source: http://aboutjapan.japansociety.org/content.cfm/uss_arizona

addition, American ships have been reported torpedoed on the high seas between San Francisco and Honolulu. Yesterday, the Japanese government also launched an attack against Malaya. Last night, Japanese forces attacked Hong Kong. Last night, Japanese forces attacked Guam. Last night, Japanese forces attacked the Philippine Islands. Last night, the Japanese attacked Wake Island. And this morning, the Japanese attacked Midway Island.

Japan has, therefore, undertaken a surprise offensive extending throughout the Pacific area. The facts of yesterday and today speak for themselves. The people of the United States have already formed their opinions and well understand the implications to the very life and safety of our nation…<u>I ask that the Congress declare that since the unprovoked and dastardly attack by Japan on Sunday, December 7th, 1941, a state of war has existed between the United States and the Japanese empire.</u>"

Congress approved the vote, and the United States officially declared war against the Empire of Japan. Four days later, Germany, an ally of Japan, declared war on the United States.

The United States had officially entered World War Two, and had the unique challenge of fighting a war on two fronts: one in Europe (against Germany and Italy) and one in the Pacific (against Japan). What did the Americans and the Allied forces do to win the war? Let's find out.

Chapter 3: What Happened During World War Two?

Once the United States had decided to join World War Two, there was no time to be lost. They had desperate enemies to fight against, and these evil people needed to be stopped.

The first priority was to halt the nearly unstoppable movement of Japan in the Pacific. The United States fought back, and the first battle was fought from May 4-8, 1942 at the Coral Sea near Australia. This war was intriguing because the enemy ships never actually saw each other. Using the new technology of radar and large aircraft carriers, they simply sent planes back and forth to attack each other's ships. Although the Japanese were able to seriously hurt the Allied forces, even killing 656 sailors and pilots, they themselves were stopped for the first time in their military campaign. The Japanese also suffered heavy losses, including 966 people killed and five ships sunk. During the next major sea battle between the Americans and the Japanese, the missing men and ships made it a more of an equal battle.

The Battle of Midway was fought from June 4-7, 1942 and was a definite American victory. The Japanese had hoped to lure the Americans into a trap and to take over the island of Midway to use as a base during the war. However, the Americans were able to intercept and decipher the coded transmissions and to figure out where the next attack would be. They were ready when the Japanese arrived, and the battle was intense. In just four short days, the Japanese lost four carriers and one cruiser, with a total of 3,057 persons killed. The Americans only lost one carrier and one destroyer, with 307 people dead.

From that moment on, the Americans were no longer defending themselves; they began to go on the offensive, pushing the Japanese fleet further and further back towards Japan.

In the meantime, American forces began to arrive and fight in Europe. On November 8, 1942, Operation Torch was carried out using American and Allied soldiers in North Africa.

American troops arrived on the beaches of North Africa on November 8, 1942.[16]

---

[16] Image source: http://en.wikipedia.org/wiki/File:Torch-troops_hit_the_beaches.jpg

The goal was to get rid of Axis soldiers in North Africa in order to gain control of the Mediterranean and to be able to invade Europe from the south, forcing Hitler to fight on two fronts (one with Russia in the north, one with the Allies in the south). The initial battle lasted about eight days, and the Allies won. The Americans had contributed to this first historic victory in the war against the Axis powers!

The Allies spent the next year fighting against Italian forces, who finally surrendered on June 4, 1944. However, the biggest contribution of the Americans to the Allied war effort took place two days later, on June 6, 1944, at an event that came to be known as "D-Day". Part of Operation Overload, on this day tens of thousands of Allied troops landed on the beaches of Normandy, France, in order to open up a massive second front in the war with Germany. As we saw in the introduction, it was a terrible struggle, and some 6,000 Americans died on the beaches that day, but their courage and bravery allowed the Allies to get a foothold in Europe and to start moving troops and supplies to fight the war there.

The soldiers then spent the next few months slowly moving inland, fighting against the German forces. Paris was liberated from Nazi control on August 25, and the Allies kept pushing the Germans further and further back towards where they came from. On December 16, the Germans tried to push back against the advancing allies and to break their lines. In this huge battle, called the Battle of the Bulge, there were eventually some 610,000 Allied soldiers, mainly American, fighting against a large German army of about 250,000 soldiers. The fighting was fierce, but by the end of the four-week battle, the Germans had lost. Some 100,000 German soldiers had died or had been wounded, compared to 89,000 American troops.

The Battle of the Bulge (named for the shape in the Allied battle lines when the Germans attacked and made them retreat) was an important turning point for many reasons. Not only did it show how dedicated the Americans were to defeating Hitler, but it also allowed African-Americans to fight on the front lines for the first time. This battle also drained Germany's reserve forces to the limit. Germany had bet everything on beating the Allies, and they had lost. It was the beginning of the end for Germany.

Meanwhile, in the Pacific, the war against the Japanese was going more and more in favor of the Allies. After winning the Battle of Midway, the Allies began to push the Japanese back towards their homeland. Instead of wasting lots of time conquering each and every one of the thousands of islands in the Pacific, it was decided that the Allies would have a campaign of "island-hopping" where they would move from one island to another, skipping the small ones, to get closer and closer to the Japanese mainland.

The United States had entered World War Two on December 8, 1942. By early 1945, they had helped to stop the Axis forces on both fronts and were pushing them back where they had come from. They were finally winning the war.

Chapter 4: What Was it Like to be a Kid During World War Two?

As we saw in the introduction, kids were not allowed to fight in the war as part of any army. However, like the rest of the world, kids knew what was going on and they were affected by it. Let's talk first about what it was like to be a kid in the U.S., and then we will talk about some of the sad stuff that kids in Europe saw.

Kids living in the United States during World War Two saw their lives get turned upside down. First off, they found that it got harder and harder to buy the food and clothing that they were used to having. Why? As raw materials (the things we use to make stuff) started to be used more and more to help the soldiers of Allied nations, there was less for the people at home. What was the solution? Ration books.

A ration book determined how much food a family could buy at the store.[17]

A ration book was assigned to each person in the family, even to the babies. It made sure that everybody could get a little bit of something (although they often wanted more). The first things to be rationed were car tires (for the rubber), but soon all kinds of things had to be rationed: coffee, sugar, meat, cheese, gasoline, butter, canned, foods, and even bicycles. Some new items (like cars and appliances) weren't even made during the war. All of the materials needed to be used to make bullets and airplanes and other things to help the soldiers fighting in the war.

As a kid living in the U.S., you would have had to eat your favorite foods less often. A lot of families decided to grow food at home, and called their gardens "Victory Gardens" or "War Gardens" because of the way they contributed to the war effort. Your mom might have asked you to go out and dig in the garden, and from time to time you may have gotten to help to pick fresh vegetables and spices.

Although there weren't too many attacks on American soil, everyone was constantly aware of the threat from both the Japanese and German armies. However, did you know that both the Japanese and Germany militaries tried to attack the United States mainland? It's true! And some kids were pretty scared when it happened.

---

[17] Image source: http://allthenutsinthetree.blogspot.com/2011_04_01_archive.html

The Japanese tried to send "balloon bombs" to the American mainland. They sewed together gargantuan balloons and filled them with hydrogen air. Then, they attached bombs to these balloons and let them go up into the Jetstream, a current of wind that goes from Japan to North America. Over 3,000 of these balloons were launched, but just a few made it to the United States, and only one claimed any victims. But can you imagine what it was like for many American kids to be afraid of a balloon bomb dropping down on them from the sky?

On the other side of the country, long range German submarines had been able to travel as all the way to New York harbor. At night, they would look out their periscopes and look for the outline of ships against the city lights. They sunk so many ships that eventually the government had to ask people to turn off their lights at night so that the submarines couldn't see the silhouettes of the boats anymore in order to sink them. Kids had to practice turning out the lights whenever the government told them to.

Also, in the United States, many kids had to spend less time with their moms. Why? Well, because many moms went to work in large factories where materials for the wars were made, like you can see in the picture below.

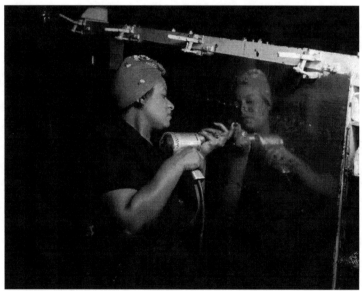

A hard-working factory worker puts in the rivets on part of a dive bomber.[18]

Kids in the United States had to think a lot about the war and wonder when their dads and brothers were coming home, or even *if* they were coming home. However, for kids in Europe (and some parts of Asia), they didn't just think about the war; they lived it every day.

Think about what it meant for kids who lived in a war zone. Many times, they had to evacuate cities as armies moved in. Sometimes their houses were destroyed by bombs, their families were arrested and sent to prison, and sometimes they had to live with foster parents or relatives after the war was over. In Europe, some innocent kids had to see some terrible things. Like what? Do you remember what Adolf Hitler wanted to do? That's right: he wanted to conquer all of Europe and to stop Communism from spreading. However, he also wanted to get rid of certain people that he saw as "undesirable", or not as good as others. Among them were Jewish people, Gypsies, handicapped people, and even certain

[18] Image source: http://en.wikipedia.org/wiki/File:Rosie_the_Riveter_(Vultee)_DS.jpg

religions like Jehovah's Witnesses, who refused to go along with what Hitler wanted. What did Hitler do with all these people?

He would round them up and take them to "work camps". At these camps, some people were forced to make clothing and weapons for the German army while others were simply executed. Even children were taken to these camps and mistreated, and sometimes they were even killed.

It's not pleasant to think about such sad things happening. It's even hard to think how the German guards and soldiers went along with Hitler. Some were too scared to say no; others actually agreed with him. What do you think: was it right of Hitler to round up people based on their background or religious beliefs and ship them by train to far away prisons, only to kill them? Of course not. Some six million people, mostly of Jewish descent, died in these camps. This period of time came to be known as The Holocaust, and we should never forget that it happened so that we can prevent something like it from happening again.

Hitler took prisoners of war and even fellow Germans to concentration camps like this one, called Auschwitz.[19]

Being a kid during World War Two was difficult in the United States, and it was an absolute nightmare in Europe.

[19] Image source: http://wp.lehman.edu/lehman-today/2012/04/lehman-professor-leads-holocaust-educators-on-visit-to-historical-sites-in-poland-and-israel/

Chapter 5: How Did World War Two End?

As we saw earlier, World War Two was being fought against two main enemies: Germany and Japan (Italy had already surrendered earlier to the Allied forces). We know that the Allies eventually won, but how did the bad guys actually lose? Let's find out.

First, let's look at Germany. As we saw, the Battle of the Bulge was a huge defeat for the German army. They had some 100,000 casualties, and they had not gained any of their objectives. The Soviets (Russians) were pushing harder and harder on the eastern flank, and Germany was soon retreating in Italy also. All of the large gains that Germany had made during the war were being lost, one step at a time, as the troops were forced to retreat over and over and over again.

On February 4, 1945, the leaders of the Allies met with Soviet leader Joseph Stalin in Ukraine to discuss what should happen to Germany after the war. It was clear that Germany was close to being stopped.

Winston Churchill, Franklin D. Roosevelt, and Joseph Stalin met together to discuss the war.[20]

It was discussed that the Soviet Union would enter the war against Japan at a future date and that Germany would be occupied by the allies after the war.

On April 30, 1945, Allied forces captured the Reichstag (the German capital building) and Adolf Hitler (hidden in a secret bunker in the same city) committed suicide by swallowing poison. Germany had been defeated, and on May 8, Germany officially signed a document of surrender. The day was declared Victory in Europe day. But the war wasn't over yet.

[20] Image source: http://en.wikipedia.org/wiki/Yalta_Conference

Let's have a look at Japan. As you may remember, the Pacific Theater had a lot of genuinely tough fighting. Huge ships used planes and large guns to attack each other, and the Allies (including the United States at The Battle of Midway) were finally able to stop the offensive of the Japanese navy and to start to push them back towards Asia.

Once they arrived at the thousands of islands that surround Japan, the Allies decided to focus on the larger ones (the islands with room for airports and military bases) that they could use to prepare for the next stage of getting closer and closer to Japan.

In January 1945, the Allies had made it to the Philippines, and by May they were in Borneo. The Allies were imagining that there would be another long war like there had been in Europe, with soldiers moving bit by bit towards the capital, fighting every step of the way. Russia made plans to invade from the north, and the Allies planned to move in from the south. However, before a full-scale invasion was started, the Allies wanted to weaken the Japanese fighting force. They did this by means of a weapon that had worked well in Europe- firebombing.

Do you know what firebombing is? A normal bomb, when dropped on a city, uses a large explosion to destroy buildings and to kill people. However, a firebomb has a smaller explosion, but its main goal is to start lots of little fires that spread across a city. The Allies wanted to burn down military bases and factories so that the Japanese would not be able to fight as well when the invasion came. Most of the large cities in Japan were firebombed, and it is estimated that hundreds of thousands of people were killed. For example, in February of 1945, some 100,000 people in Tokyo alone died as a result of firebombing. It was a scary time.

The Empire of Japan was still fighting and would not surrender. Before launch the invasion that they had planned, the United States decided to use a brand new bomb that they had been secretly developing. It was called the Atomic Bomb. The Atomic Bomb used a new type of technology to create larger and deadlier explosions and shockwaves, and the covered the area with radiation afterwards.

The two atomic bombs dropped in Japan made immense mushroom clouds.[21]

The United States was sure that dropping these incredibly damaging bombs would help convince Japan to surrender quickly. They knew that the destructive would scare a lot of people and that the psychological (emotional) effect would be even more effective than the destruction. The target cities were based on size and usefulness. Eventually, two bombs were dropped in 1945, on the cities of Hiroshima (August 6) and Nagasaki (on August 9). The Allies wanted unconditional surrender from Japan, and they finally received it on August 15.

World War Two had been fought and won by the Allies. The violence and pain were finally over.

---

[21] Image source: http://en.wikipedia.org/wiki/File:Atomic_bombing_of_Japan.jpg

Chapter 6: What Happened After World War Two?

Once the fighting had stopped, the world needed to start to heal. Cities needed to be rebuilt, the dead needed to be buried, and the world needed to make sure that Germany would not be a threat again. The first main problem was what to do with Germany.

The Allies decided that Germany would have to be occupied for some time by foreign troops until a stable, friendly government could be established. It was decided that the Soviet Union would occupy the eastern part of Germany and the rest of the allies the western part. In time, two remarkably different Germany's emerged: a democratic Germany in the west and a communist Germany in the east. This strange creation, a country split into two parts, would last throughout the next forty-plus years.

In order to prevent something as terrible as World War Two (and the Holocaust) from ever happening again, the Allied forces held trials to prosecute and execute the leadership of Nazi Germany. Although Adolf Hitler and a few other high-ranking officials had committed suicide, others were taken to trial, sentenced, and executed for the horrible things that they had done.

In Asia, Japan had agreed to a total surrender, so the lands that they had conquered were given back to the original owners. China, now no longer worrying about war with Japan, experienced a civil war and became a communist nation. The country of Korea found itself in a position remarkably similar to that of Germany- it was divided into two parts, and one (the northern part) became communist and the other (the southern part) democratic. The tensions became strong, and an awful war would erupt in that tiny peninsula in 1950.

Although the League of Nations, an international group of ambassadors meant to prevent world war, had failed to prevent World War Two, many people still felt optimistic that the countries of the world could solve their problems without war if they just had a place to get together and talk things out. As a result, on October 24, 1945, the United Nations was formed in order to prevent a third world war from breaking out, and so far it has been successful.

World War Two left a total of some 60 million people dead. Can you even imagine such a large number? At the time, it was about two out of every one hundred people dying. It would be as if the entire population of the United Kingdom disappeared, or if everyone in the states of California and New York suddenly died. After so much death, the world needed time to heal.

However, the construction of the atomic bomb made a lot of governments realize how fast a war could be fought. They realized how many people could be killed in a matter of minutes. The next few decades saw the Unites States and the USSR (Russia) start to race to build stronger and better bombs, just in case a war broke out. The Cold War, as it was called, would last until the early 1990s.

Conclusion

This has been a truly fascinating handbook because it's let us learn about one of the most pivotal times in human history- a time when almost the entire world was at war with each other. A lot of terrible things happened, and a lot of people died. However, some seriously bad people were stopped, and a lot of lives were saved.

Do you remember all of the interesting things that we learned? Let's review. First, we looked at what led up to the outbreak of World War Two. We saw how three separate nations, Italy, Germany, and Japan, all got together in order see how they could make their countries larger and more powerful. Although Japan had invaded China a few years earlier, most historians feel that World War Two actually started with Adolf Hitler's invasion of Poland in 1939. The United States tried to stay neutral at first, and then they tried to just give money and weapons to the Allied forces.

Then, we learned about the event that made the United States formally enter the war. Do you remember what that event was? It was the bombing of Pearl Harbor on December 7, 1941. The Japanese had wanted to make sure that the Americans wouldn't get in their way as they tried to take over Asia, so they launched a massive attack against the American naval ships stationed at Pearl Harbor, in Hawaii. A lot of people died, but the Navy was able to repair many of the ships and get back out into the ocean to fight against the Japanese. Their first job was to get the ships up and running again to stop Japan, and then to get troops over to Europe to fight against Italy and Germany.

After that, we saw how the United States fought in World War Two on two separate fronts: in the European Theater and in the Pacific Theater. The Pacific Theater was all about naval warfare, and the world got to see massive groups of ships sending planes back and forth to sink each other. After the historic Battle of Midway, the United States gained the upper hand and began to push the Japanese back towards their home island. From there, the battle changed to "island hopping", moving closer and closer to the mainland.

In Europe, after landing in Africa and pushing north into Europe, the Allies helped to defeat Italy and start pushing the Germany army northwards. Meanwhile, with the massive invasion of troops on D-Day, a second front was created (in addition to the one with Russia) and Hitler had to fight a two-front war. After a series of victories, culminating in the Battle of the Bulge, Hitler's armies started a long retreat back to Berlin, the capital of Germany. The war was starting to go in favor of the Allies.

The next section talked about what it was like to be a kid back then. Although no kids were allowed to fight in World War Two on either side, they were affected by what was going on. Things at home changed, and even school and meals were affected. We also saw how kids had to practice blackouts (to help ships avoid getting sunk by submarines) and had to ration their food. We also learned about some of the terrible things that kids in Europe saw like the people killed by the Holocaust. It was a sad time.

The following section talked about something more positive: the end of World War Two. We saw what events finally led to the end of this global conflict, both in Europe and then in the Pacific. Do you remember what they were? In Europe, the Battle of the Bulge was the last time that the German army tried to push back the advancing Allies and to break their battle lines. Although they came close, the large number of fresh American troops was finally too much, and the Germans had to retreat. Soon, Hitler committed suicide, and the Germans surrendered.

In the Pacific, we learned how effective the island hopping campaign was. It allowed the Allied forces to get remarkably close to the Japanese mainland. Bombers weakened the large cities, and finally two atomic bombs were dropped. After seeing the destructive new weapons, the Japanese surrendered unconditionally. The war had finally ended.

Finally, we saw what happened after the war ended, including both the short-term and long-term consequences of the war. Some of the short term consequences had to do with rebuilding Europe and Asia and helping to punish the people that had caused so much trouble. Some of the long-term consequences involved forming a dual-power Germany and Korea, both of which became supremely important issues during the Cold War that followed.

World War Two was a time when the entire world was at war, and their governments, industries, and citizens all got together to support the war effort. Over 60 million people died, and we should never forget their sacrifice. If you know someone who fought in or was affected by World War Two, why not ask them about it?

If you know a veteran of World War Two, why not ask them about their experience?[22]

[22] Image source: http://dav44.org/

Korean War

One American soldier comforts another whose best friend was just killed in the fighting.[23]

---

[23] Image source: http://authorgarywilliams.net/?p=662

Introduction

Platoon Sergeant Daniel Adams ducked his head down to avoid the bullets that seemed to be coming from everywhere. To his right, a massive explosion rocked the earth and sent dirt flying in all directions. Daniel was pretty sure that he heard some screaming in English, but he couldn't be sure. Through the smoke and dust, it was hard to see much of anything, and it was harder still to know who exactly he was fighting against or where they were shooting from. He heard some more gunshots from up ahead and to the left, and ducked his head back behind the rocks that protected him.

One week ago, Daniel had been stationed in Japan, helping the country recuperate from the damage of World War Two. Then he had heard on the news that the North Korean military had sent soldiers down across the border to South Korea and that there was a lot of fighting. Daniel knew that he and his infantry unit had been sent here, to Osan, south of the capital of Seoul, to stop the advancing North Korean army. But he and his fellow soldiers weren't prepared at all to fight against tanks and artillery, both of which the North Korean army had. The Americans only had guns, no tanks and no heavy weapons.

Another round was fired from a tank; Daniel could tell by the louder boom, and he curled into a ball. The earth around him exploded, and he knew that the shell had landed just a few feet from his current position. He popped up from behind the rock and fired towards where the shell came from. The men on either side of him did the same. In the hot weather, they never stopped sweating, not even at night. They had no supplies, and they were drinking the dirty water used to irrigate rice fields. Daniels stomach had cramped up yesterday as a result, but the North Koreans sure weren't about to wait for him to feel better before attacking.

Daniel's men looked at each other through the smoke and the dust. In his Infantry Regiment, there were about 500 soldiers. The wind picked up for a moment and Daniel could see over to where the enemy was, and the sight took his breath away. There were more than 500 soldiers, many more. He saw row after row of tanks, and men lined up as far back as his eye could see. His immediate superior, his platoon leader, Lieutenant Dodgson, yelled out: "There's gotta be at least 5,000 of them, and a few dozen tanks! We won't be able to hold them off forever! What do they expect us to do out here?"

Daniel looked over at his Platoon Leader and couldn't believe it- he heard fear in the man's voice! Looking into the Lieutenant's eyes, Daniel yelled back: "Sir, we have to hold. Those were our orders. We have to fight to the last man."

The Lieutenant kept staring at the tanks. He yelled over the sound of the fighting. "We can't stop those tanks, Sergeant Adams. We don't have the firepower. My radio's down, and I can't get through to the Captain." He looked behind him, then to the right and to the left. "No, we have to fall back. The rest of the regiment must have already retreated; that's the only explanation for the radio silence. It's been three hours, the odds are getting worse, and we've got no air support out here. We're alone, and we don't stand a chance. Give the order to fall back, Sergeant Adams. Give it now."

Daniel took a breath and then shouted out: "Fall back, fall back, right now. Leave your heavy equipment. Take only what you can carry and get going. Fall back now!"

The men of Company B looked almost grateful to finally be moving away from the advancing North Korean troops. They moved back towards a clump of trees where the wounded were being treated. As he bent down in order to pick up a litter that held a wounded soldier, the Lieutenant Dodgson told him, "No time, Adams. There's no time. Leave him with the medic. The North Koreans know the rules of the U.N. charter: that all prisoners of war must be treated with dignity. And they know that noncombatant personnel, like the medic here, cannot be hurt either. Leave them, there's no time."

Daniel froze, unsure what to do, and looked into the eyes of the medic. The medic seemed sad, but shook his head. "Go, Adams. We'll be fine."

Daniels grabbed his gun and ran, with the rest of his men, south, away from the North Korean soldiers.

He never saw the medic or the wounded soldier again.

Can you imagine what it would have been like to have been fighting in that battle? Called the Battle of Osan, it was fought on July 6, 1950, and marked the first armed intervention of American soldiers in the Korean War. The story we saw above actually happened, although the characters weren't real. Company B, part of the 1st Battalion, 21st Infantry of the United States Army, certainly was left behind when the rest of the troops retreated, and they had to leave behind their equipment and their wounded in order to get away safely. It was a scary battle.

Have you ever heard of the Battle of Osan, or even of the Korean War that it was a part of? This war has been called America's "Forgotten War" because not a lot of people talk about it. It was not global, like World War Two had been, and it was not as controversial as the Vietnam War. Although it lasted for about three years, and although some 40,000 American soldiers lost their lives, the whole thing seemed so far away that, to this day, not a lot of people even know what the war was about or how it ended. Sometimes, they don't even know that it happened. In this handbook, we hope that you will learn the most pertinent stuff about the Korean War. What can you expect to see?

First, we will learn more about what actually caused the Korean War. Did you know that the war actually started as a sort of civil war between the Korean people but that later other nations got involved? Also, do you know what the Korean War has to do with the Cold War that was fought between the United States and the U.S.S.R.? You will learn the answers in this section.

The next section will talk more about why the United States and other nations got involved in the civil war of a nation on the other side of the world. One of the biggest reasons was something called the "domino theory", something that genuinely scared the President of the United States. We will also learn what the U.S.S.R. and China thought about the United States getting involved in the war, and what they did about it.

After that, we will learn more about the Korean War itself. As you can see in the picture at the beginning of this handbook, there were some truly sad moments during the war, like when soldiers lost their best friends on the battlefields. The Korean War also saw a lot of soldiers and civilians get killed, and you may be surprised to find out who was responsible for many of the deaths.

The following section will tell us what it was like to be a kid living during the Korean War. We will use our imaginations to see what it was like to be a kid in the United States during the war, and what kinds of things they would have seen and heard about. Then we will see what it would have been like to be a kid living in Korea during the war. As you can probably imagine, it would have been a lot scarier in Korea!

After that, we will see how the Korean War finally ended. Although the fighting was pretty fierce and tough in the beginning, and although the armies moved around a lot, by the end of the war, things had settled down and everyone wanted the fighting to end. Even so, it took almost two years for the governments on each side to finally sign the documents that ended the fighting. We will see what conditions were finally met to stop the bullets from flying and the bombs from being dropped.

The section after that will let us know what it was like after the war ended, and will include some of the final facts and figures.

Before we read any further, you may wonder why you should care about a war that happened over 60 years ago. Well, in many ways, the causes of that war are still around, and a lot of people are worried that another war in Korea could break out anytime. As you probably know, the only way to avoid repeating the mistakes of the past is to learn from them. So try to learn what the factors were which led to so many people dying in the Korean War. That way, maybe we can keep the same thing from happening again in the future.

The Korean War was fought from June 25, 1950 to July 27, 1953. Let's learn more about this sad but significant war.

Chapter 1: What Led Up to the Korean War?

A young Korean girl with her baby brother walks by a tank during the Korean War.[24]

Why did the Korean peninsula erupt in civil war in 1953? Basically, the country was split into two halves after World War Two, and there was a fight as to which way the reestablished government should be run. But how did the country get to be split into two halves in the first place? Let's find out.

In 1910, the nearby island empire of Japan decided to invade and conquer the land of Korea. Until World War Two, the Korean people were totally ruled by the Empire of Japan, and they had no voice at all in the way that their government was run or in the way that they were treated. Once World War Two broke out, the Japanese used the Koreans to make their country stronger, and many Koreans were forced to go to Japanese cities and to work on behalf of the war effort. When the two atomic bombs were dropped on the cities of Hiroshima and Nagasaki in 1945, about 25% of all the people who died were Koreans that had been forced to support the Japanese war machine.

During the war, the Soviet Union (U.S.S.R.) had agreed to step in and to help the Allied forces stop Japan from taking over Asia. The Soviets moved in from the north, closer and closer to Japan, and made it all the way to the 38th Parallel (a circle of latitude marking a location) of the Korean peninsula, deep into Japanese territory. Once there, they waited for further instructions and to see how the Allied invasion of Japan went.

Once the war was over, it was decided by representatives in Washington D.C. that Korea would need some help getting on its feet and establishing itself as an independent nation again. After all, the country had been dominated by a foreign country for over 30 years. It was decided that the Soviets would care for the northern part of Korean down to the 38th Parallel, and the Allied forces (principally the United States) would take care of everything from there south.

[24] Image source: http://www.archives.gov/research/military/korean-war/

World War Two ended towards the final part of 1945, and the occupation by the Soviets and the Allies followed almost immediately afterwards. The citizens of Korea had the same problems to handle as those of any country, but because of the foreign influences, the northern part and the southern part decided to handle their problems very differently. Although both sides wanted to be united together again as one nation, the northern part favored a Communist government (like the U.S.S.R.) while the southern side favored a Democratic form of government (like the U.S.A.).

Before we continue, let's talk a moment about the different between a "Communist" and a "Democratic" government. In a democratic government, like in the United States, the people have a lot more say in what and how things are done. They can decide which laws they want, who should be in charge, and they can elect representatives who will decide whether or not to go to war and with whom. Citizens can choose where to work, large companies can compete with each other, and individuals can buy and own houses and properties. A Democratic government responds to the people, and so it always tries to be fair and to do the right thing.

A Communist government is also for the people, but it is set up a little differently. Instead of establishing private companies and private property, the idea is that everything belongs to the community. Everyone shares the good that the community produces, and they receive from the community (represented by a small government) a house, a job, and enough food for their family. However, Communism looks good on paper (because everyone gets what they need), but it becomes extremely easy for a few bad guys to take advantage of it. Also, because there can be lots of problems organizing everything, this type of government tends to cause a lot of suffering and poverty in the countries that accept it.

You can understand that both halves of Korea, the Communist Northern part and the Democratic Southern part, both thought that their form of government was the best. However, some people living in the North wanted things to be more like the South, and vice versa. The governments of both sides were particularly mean to the citizens who didn't agree with them, and many were executed if they tried to protest or change the way things were done.

The border between the two sides, the 38th Parallel, became the focal point of fighting and tensions between the two sides, because it was where one way of doing things ended and another began. In the years after World War Two ended, there were lots of little fights (called skirmishes) between Northern and Southern soldiers, and lots of people died. It is estimated that about 10,000 soldiers had died by the time the Korean War "officially" started.

The world was taking notice of the fighting going on between the two parts of Korea, but there were two nations in particular that were truly interested: the United States of America (U.S.A.) and the Union of Soviet Socialist Republics (U.S.S.R.). After World War Two ended, both sides looked at each other with a lot of suspicion. Because the United States thought that everybody should have a democratic government and because the Soviets thought that everybody should have a communist government, the two sides both thought that the other was about to start a war. They started building up their piles of weapons and getting ready for a fight. This came to be known as the Cold War. It was "cold" because there was no direct fighting between the two nations; just a lot of threats and spies and secret plans.

Both the U.S.S.R. and the U.S.A. felt that Korea should be united as one country, but they couldn't agree if it should be a democratic government or a communist one. Even though everyone got together to talk about peace and finding a solution, things worked out kind of differently. On June 25, 1950, tons of North Korean troops marched across the 38th Parallel towards Seoul, the capital city of South Korea.

They decided that enough time had been spent in talking and that it was time for action. Although there had been lots of little fights before, this one was gigantic, and lots of soldiers were involved.

Two days later, on the 27th of June, the President of South Korea (Syngman Rhee) fled the capital city and established a new headquarters in the southern city of Busan. The next day, the 28th of June, saw a lot of Korean blood spilled onto the streets. The North Korean army arrived in Seoul, and among the many violent acts they carried out was a massacre of 900 doctors, nurses, patients, and wounded soldiers at a hospital in Seoul. For his part, President Syngman Rhee ordered that mass executions of suspected Communists and friends of Communists be carried out. Within just a few months, over 100,000 South Koreans, his fellow citizens, had been killed. It is sad to say, but that number includes many young children and innocent civilians. The bodies were buried in large graves, some of which have still not been found today.

On that same day, President Syngman Rhee ordered that a main bridge leading into Seoul be blown up in order to hold back the North Korean troops that were trying to enter. But there was a problem: the bridge was full of South Korean citizens trying to escape the Communist troops and to head further south. The South Korean army didn't warn anyone about the destruction of the bridge, and they blew it up at 2:30 PM on June 28, when there were more than 4,000 refugees walking across it. Over 800 people died in the blast and in the bridge collapse, and part of the South Korean army was trapped on the other side.

June 28 was a day when a lot of Korean blood was spilled on the ground, entirely by other Koreans. The question was: how much longer would the killing go on?

As you may know, after World War Two was finished, a special organization was set up: The United Nations. This organization was to be a place where governments could get together to talk about their problems without having to go to war. What did the United Nations think about the North Korean army's invasion of the South? They condemned it and sent troops (made up mostly of Americans, along with some British, Canadian, and Australian soldiers) to stop the fighting and to unite the peninsula. On June 27, 1950, the Security Council of the United Nations passed resolution 83, which included the following statement:

> "[The Security Council] recommends that the Members of the United Nations furnish such assistance to the Republic of Korea as may be necessary to repel the armed attack and to restore international peace and security in the area.[25]"

Meanwhile, the U.S.S.R. decided that it would secretly help the Communist North to win, while the Allies (mainly made up of Americans) decided that they would go and fight for the Democratic South.

The international community had officially become a part of the Korean War.

---

[25] Image source: http://www.unhcr.org/refworld/docid/3b00f20a2c.html

Chapter 2: Why Did the Korean War Happen?

Have you ever played with a set of dominos? Well, what happens if you line them all up and then push over the one at the end? You would probably see something like the following happen:

One single domino that falls can trigger a chain reaction and make all the dominos fall.[26]

A lot of people around the world thought that Korea was like a domino. How so? Well, do you remember the tensions that existed between the U.S.S.R. and the United States? The United States didn't want Communism to spread to any more countries, and the U.S.S.R. thought that lots of countries should try this new type of government. In fact, the civil war in China that had been fought just after World War Two ended up bringing in a Communist government. The United States, along with some other countries, was worried that if Korea became a Communist country than other nearby Asian lands would also, and maybe all of Europe would, as well.

The world had seen that while Communism had the goal of helping people, the citizens were the ones who often ended up suffering. For example, in 1932 the Soviet Union experienced a terrible famine, during which some six million Soviets died as a result of not having enough food. The government had not been able to manage the Communist system well, and the farmers themselves had to give away all the food that they grew to people living in the big cities. The farmers were often left with nothing for themselves. The United States was worried that if Communism were to spread, then many more people would be forced to suffer like those Soviets had during the famine.

[26] Image source: http://insureblog.blogspot.com/2012/07/dominos-part-deux.html

The goal of the United States, as stated exceptionally clearly by President Truman, became one of "containment", or in other words, of keeping the Soviets from gaining any new ground in the future or from spreading their politics to other countries. When the Korean War broke out, Truman was afraid that the Soviets were going to try to get Korea united under a Communist government and that they would then move on to Japan, which had become a new stronghold and base for Democracy in Asia.

It was also feared that the war in Korea would get larger and larger, eventually becoming a global conflict (like what had happened in World War One). It was hoped that by the United Nations getting involved early in the fighting then other nations (like China and the U.S.S.R.) wouldn't get involved and make the whole thing get bigger than it had to be.

Truman initially referred to the U.N. intervention in the Korean civil war as a "police action". It was hoped that the fighting would be minimal, and it would be more like a teacher trying to break up a fight between two boys on the playground. Also, Truman thought that this war, if it was allowed to escalate and involve a lot of other nations, would become a threat to the young organization of the United Nations. After all, if no one took what the U.N. said seriously when talking about a small war in Asia, how would it ever be able to prevent a Third World War?

As you can see, what started as a fight between the two halves of one country quickly became something much larger. The Americans thought that the Soviets were trying to expand their politics into neighboring countries, and the Soviets thought that the Americans were too blinded by their own prejudices and greed to see that there were many ways of doing things. The Soviets also thought that the Americans wanted to conquer the whole world. Although neither side was ready for a direct war, it soon became clear that they would use Korea as a sort of "proxy war". Do you know what a proxy war is?

A proxy is like a representative. Sometimes, when an executive has to vote in an important company meeting, but he can't make it, he will send a "proxy" to vote for him. So a proxy war is when two countries use representatives (other armies) to fight their war for them. The Soviets used the North Koreans, and the Americans used the South Koreans. Both sides gave money, supplies, and advice to the armies, and the Americans even sent thousands of soldiers to Korea to fight.

This proxy war never escalated to become a Third World War, but that doesn't mean that it was an unimportant war. It was important to the world and to the Korean people. In fact, what do you think the Korean people thought about the Soviets and the Americans using them like chess pieces?

Do you remember how there was a lot of fighting just before the war broke out? Thousands of Koreans died because they couldn't get along. Some wanted a Communist government and others wanted a democratic government. Normally, the best way to decide something is for everyone to get together and talk about it or vote on it in a free election. However, the foreign power that was occupying the northern part of the Korean Peninsula (the U.S.S.R.) didn't allow free elections in 1948. The people had been ruled for thirty years by the Japanese, were never listened to, and now it felt like history was repeating itself.

In fact, when the decision was made for the Soviets, and the Americans to occupy the two halves of Korea guess how many Koreans they asked about it? None! That's right. Even in that pivotal moment when the future of Korea would be decided, the Korean people still were not able to have a voice in the decision!

As a result, even though the south was officially "Democratic", that didn't mean that everyone was 100% on board with the decisions made by the president. And in the North, some people didn't want the Soviets pushing them around; but they actually didn't have a choice in the matter.

When the fighting finally started in June of 1950, the soldiers on each side were scared, but some were more prepared than others for the long months and years of fighting that awaited them.

Chapter 3: What Happened During the Korean War?

An American soldier sits on a captured hill during a quiet moment of the Korean War in 1951.[27]

As we have seen already, the Korean War started with a day of horrific violence. Men, women, and children were gunned down by their fellow citizens, and it seemed like there was no escape. Wherever the citizens turned, especially near the capital, it seemed like there were explosions, gunshots, and screams of pain and sadness. When the United Nations authorized the Americans and others to intervene, it was hoped that the arrival of more forces would calm things down in the region and help to stabilize the peninsula. Unfortunately, when the help finally arrived, it was too little, too late.

The first American troops were quickly moved over from nearby Japan, and they soon arrived in Korea on July 1. The first battle of the Korean War that included American soldiers was on July 5, 1950, near the city of Osan, south of the capital city of Seoul. There were a little more than 500 American soldiers, and their job was mainly to hold the line to keep the North Korean troops from moving further south. The Americans didn't want to lose complete control of the southern part of the peninsula and were hoping to land more troops there soon. The soldiers that fought in the Battle of Osan were from the 1st Battalion, 21st Infantry of the United States Army.

The men of the 1st Battalion, 21st Infantry were not fully prepared for the war (in terms of equipment and experience) and they were too few to be fighting against such a large amount of enemy combatants. In fact, five out of every six soldiers had never fired a weapon in war. When the giant North Korean army came out to meet them with 36 tanks and 5,000 infantry, the American soldiers were only able to hold out for about three hours before receiving the order to evacuate as we saw in the introduction. Some of the soldiers didn't get the order in time, and they had to leave behind their heavy weapons (which were later used against them) and their wound comrades in order to escape.

27 Image source: http://en.wikipedia.org/wiki/File:Korean_War_HA-SN-98-07010.jpg

The Battle of Osan made the Americans realize that they were dealing with a large, well-equipped and well-organized enemy. This was not going to be an easy walk in the park; this was going to be a difficult war.

The soldiers arrived in July, during what was to be a terribly hot summer. There was not enough water, so the men had to drink the irrigation water from nearby rice fields, water that had been contaminated with human waste. Many of the soldiers got sick, and it was hard for them to fight well. As for the South Korean soldiers themselves, many of them were also scared and inexperienced on the battlefield. For a time, it seemed like the North Koreans were going to win practically without a fight. In fact, one of the men high up in the North Korean government predicted that they would have a complete victory by November.

By August, the American soldiers (and their allies from the United Nations) had been pushed all the way down to Nakdong River, near the city of Pusan. The North Korean troops now were in control of about 90% of the peninsula and were closing in fast. The Americans decided that it was time to push back.

The first step was to stop the North Korean war machine that was marching unstoppably forward. The United States Air Force used jet-fighters to bomb enemy positions, to destroy railroads and bridges, and to keep the troops from advancing. Then, tanks and soldiers were sent directly to Korea from the United States, and by early September, the Americans and their allies outnumbered the North Korean army about 180,000 to 100,000. Things were finally starting to look like they would start going in favor of the South Korean government and the U.N. soldiers.

On September 15, a large-scale offensive was launched to the north, almost 100 miles behind the North Korean battle lines. With support from naval ships and the air force, General Douglas MacArthur (the American General in charge of the Korean War) landed some 40,000 troops onto the beach of Inchon. During four days, these soldiers killed about 1,350 North Korean troops and started a massive retreat.

Some 40,000 soldiers and tanks participated in the Battle of Inchon.[28]

With the rest of the army pushing up from the south, the North Korean soldiers were soon retreating in a thoroughly disorganized way, leaving many men behind and even leaving their capital city, Pyongyang, vulnerable. On September 25, Seoul was recaptured by the Americans and South Korean forces.

The fight kept moving further and further north, and on October 7, the Americans and their allies crossed the 38th Parallel, officially in enemy territory. China had previously threatened that it would be upset and would try to stop the Americans if that happened, but their warnings weren't actually listened to. As we will see, China was about to get involved and change the way the war was fought.

The American soldiers kept pushing further and further north, and it looked as if the war might end soon, with a victory for the Democratic South. However, as American troops neared the Chinese border, they were surprised to learn that some two hundred thousand Chinese troops had crossed the border and were fighting for the North Koreans. On October 25, 1950, the Chinese troops had entered Korea. They, like the North Koreans, were supported by a Communist government. The three nations shared the same political ideas, and now they shared the same enemy. Although not everyone in the Chinese government wanted war with the United States, the most powerful people (including Premier Zhou Enlai) did, and so China entered the war.

General MacArthur had thought that the Chinese would never enter the war, and that if they did they would be slaughtered by the Air Force. But the Chinese used tactics to avoid being seen by the Americans. They only marched at night, used camouflage during the day, and froze in place whenever a plane flew overhead. As a result, the Chinese entered by surprise and on November 1 they were able to fight against and push back the U.S. soldiers before retreating back into the mountains. In a series of offensives, the Chinese and the North Koreans were able to, time after time, push the Americans and U.N. soldiers all the way down south, past the city of Seoul.

During the month of December, the American and South Korean troops were the ones retreating. During one mass evacuation in December, one boat, built to carry 12 passengers, carried over 14,000 refugees to safety, without losing a single one of them to the bullets being shot by North Korea soldiers. The *SS Meredith Victory* holds the record for the largest single evacuation by one ship, and many thousands of innocent people's lives were saved by the bravery of the men sailing that ship.

During an especially strong offensive, the city of Seoul was officially recaptured by the North Koreans on January 4. At this moment, General MacArthur started seriously thinking about using nuclear weapons against the North Korean and Chinese troops. He thought that it might bring a quick end to the war, just as the atom bombs had in Japan during World War Two. The President of the United States didn't agree, but MacArthur thought that since he was the General on the field of battle it was his decision.

During the next few months, the Americans and their allies got better organized, and the North Koreans and Chinese started to have problems getting enough food for their troops. In March of 1951, the Americans and United Nations troops pushed strongly northwards and were able to take back, once again the city of Seoul. In case you are counting, you will see that this makes four times in one year that the city was conquered. The people living there were seriously suffering, and there were only about 200,000 citizens still there (down from around 1.5 million before the war).

[28] Image source: http://en.wikipedia.org/wiki/Battle_of_Inchon

When the fighting began to increase again, the Chinese started to make plans to get their Air Force in the action (something that they soon did). The fighting then began to be in the ground and in the air. On April 11, 1951, General MacArthur, who had fought on several occasions with President Truman, was fired from his position and sent to be tried in Washington D.C. He was found guilty of having disobeyed the orders of the President and of bringing China into the war by rushing past the 38th Parallel, even though China had warned the Americans not to do so.

MacArthur had felt that complete victory was the only option, even if it meant a long and costly land war in Asia, even if the war was to be against China. Truman, on the other hand, felt that it would be better to finish the "police action" that they had started: stop the fighting and start an orderly withdrawal of troops. The new General, General Matthew Ridgeway wanted to cooperate with the United Nations, and like President Truman, he wanted to limit the fighting and death and to get the troops home.

By the end of May, the troops had pushed as far north as the 38th Parallel. There, neither side could seem to get the other to budge. After all the fighting, the death, the advances and the retreats, both armies were back where they had started before the war.

Chapter 4: What Was It Like to Be a Kid During the Korean War?

The Korean War saw a lot of terrible things happen to a lot of people. There were innocent people that were killed in the streets or out in the fields, and some were either left in the hot sun or buried in giant pits with thousands of other people. Some of the people killed were even as young as twelve or thirteen years old. What do you think it was like to be a kid back then?

Being a kid in the United States would not have been too much different than now. The strange thing is that not a lot of people talked about the war or wanted to know much about what was going on over in Korea. You see, the American people had just experienced the long, drawn out horror of World War Two. They had been scared of being attacked by Japanese or German submarines, and had even started to get suspicious of Japanese and German people who were American citizens. After the war had ended, everyone kind of wanted to forget about it and move on, just get on with their lives.

When the United Nations Security Council decided to send troops to Korea, several thousand young men went. But the Korean War never had the support of the whole country like World War Two did. It all seemed so far away and hard to understand. It wasn't as easy to grasp like the other war had been, where everyone wanted revenge for Pearl Harbor or to stop Adolf Hitler. This war just seemed unimportant.

As a result, a lot of kids in the United States never quite understood what the war was all about, and there were no grandiose parades or celebrations when it was all over.

Being a kid in Korea would have been totally different.

An American soldier says hello to a Korean child during the war.[29]

As a kid living in Korea during the war, you would have your entire world get ripped apart at the seams. You would have seen neighbors with certain political ideas marched off to be executed, and you would have seen your hometown get destroyed by bombs and guns. All kinds of strange people would be marching down the roads, and it would be hard to know who the good guys were and who the bad guys were.

There wouldn't be enough food for everyone, and you would probably see your parents go hungry just so that they could give food to you and your brothers and sisters. Can you imagine seeing the sadness in their eyes as they wondered what the next day would be like?

Being a kid during the Korean War meant a lot of confusion and a lot of questions without answers, no matter where you lived.

Chapter 5: How Did the Korean War End?

By summer of 1951, the soldiers were back at the 38th Parallel, fighting each other with everything they had. Because neither army could make the other one move, they dug trenches and began to fight like the soldiers had fought back in World War One- shooting lots of bullets and bombs at each other, trying to weaken the other side.

Around that time, both sides started to get together to make some sort of a peace agreement, or at least a cease-fire. The main issue that was so hard for them to agree on was what to do with the prisoners of war. Some felt that the prisoners of war should stay where they were at while others felt that the prisoners should be forced to go back to where they came from. It was difficult, because some families had been separated, and they might never get to see each other again.

Another question was what to do with the dead soldiers. Should they be buried where they died, should they be taken home, or should everyone just forget about them? It took some time and lots of meetings, but an armistice (a long term cease-fire while a treaty can be signed) was arranged for and agreed to on July 27, 1953. Some three years after the fighting had started, it was finally about to stop.

An armistice that ended the fighting was signed on July 27, 1953.[30]

The armistice was to ensure that there would be no more fighting, but also that the prisoners of war and dead soldiers could be taken care of. During Operation Big Switch, which began in August, all prisoners of war were exchanged, and they finally got to go back home. Then, during Operation Glory, which began in July of 1954, the remains of fallen soldiers were exchanged and buried with the dignity that they deserved.

[30] Image source: http://www.nationaljournal.com/pictures-video/nearly-60-years-after-armistice-korean-war-hasn-t-ended-pictures-20120727

The division of Korea was made permanent, and two independent nations, one Communist and one Democratic, were formed. In between them, there was designated a special area called a DMZ, or demilitarized zone (about 2.5 miles wide), that was to act as a sort of buffer between the two nations and to help make sure they didn't start fighting again.

North Korean soldiers look south from the DMZ.[31]

So far, although the armistice was meant to be a temporary halt to the fighting until a treaty could be signed, it has lasted almost sixty years, and no substantial fighting has broken out.

---

[31] Image source: http://en.wikipedia.org/wiki/File:JointSecurityAreaNorthKoreans.jpg

Chapter 6: What Happened After the Korean War?

The armistice that ended the fighting of the Korean War was signed on July 27, 1953. Some 40,000 American soldiers died, and another 100,000 were wounded. South Korea lost 46,000 soldiers and about 100,000 were wounded. But their losses were small compared with the enemy's. North Korea lost 215,000 troops and another 303,000 were wounded while China lost 400,000 soldiers on the battlefield, and another 486,000 were wounded. When you factor in the civilians who died and those who had to flee their homes because of the war, we can see that there was a lot of tragedy and death during the Korean War.

What has happened in Korea since the fighting stopped?

Although no substantial fighting has broken out since then, both the North and the South have been guilty of starting smaller skirmishes. One that got a lot of worldwide attention happened in 2010, when a North Korean torpedo destroyed a South Korean ship, killing 46 sailors. Because the Northern country has established the reputation of being somewhat reckless and aggressive, the whole world seems to hold its breath whenever events like that happen, wondering if another war is about to break out.

North Korea seems terribly interested in developing powerful rocket engines, which some worry may be the next step towards missiles that can be aimed at targets on the other side of the world. North Korea continues to ignore instructions and threats from the United Nations and continues to stay close to fellow Communist government, China. Time will tell if anything substantial happens in that region in the future.

South Korea, on the other hand, has recovered exceptionally well and is one of the world's largest economies and has a supremely high standard of living.

Surprisingly, some Americans defected (went to the enemy) during the Korean War. 21 American soldiers who had been captured as prisoners of war decided to stay with their captors and start new lives, mainly in China. Although their reasons were all different, some of them decided to stay for love after having met and married a local girl. Others changed their politics and actively supported Communism, never returning to the United States.

When the American soldiers came back home after having fought in the Korean War, some of them were surprised to find that there were no parades, no welcome parties, no visits to the White House to thank them for their service. They had fought for years, and it was like no one even knew what they had been doing or why they had been fighting. As we saw in the first picture, there were men crying because their best friends had died, but they came home to a country that didn't know anything about the sacrifices of them or their fellow soldiers. Can you imagine how they felt? Would you have felt appreciated?

Today, the Korean War is often called the "Forgotten War". Why? Most people don't know much about it, why it happened or who was involved. They don't understand the domino theory or how close the world got to seeing more nuclear bombs used during wartime. Worst of all, they don't realize how many Americans died fighting for the rights of others.

Conclusion

Have you learned something about the Korean War from this handbook? Could you explain it to someone else if they asked you about the war? Let's review some of the main points that we learned.

First, we learned more about what actually caused the Korean War. Did you see how the war actually started as a sort of civil war between the Korean people, but that later other nations got involved? The country had been divided into two parts after World War Two, each one occupied by a foreign power. The north was occupied by the Soviets, and the south by the Americans. When the civil war broke out, it was as if the U.S.A. and the U.S.S.R. were fighting each other through proxies, or representatives. This was one of the first battles of the Cold War.

The next section talked about why the United States and other nations got involved in the civil war of Korea, a nation on the other side of the world. Once North Korea invaded the south, the United Nations got involved and sent troops to stop the fighting, like police officers trying to calm down a rowdy crowd. The United States in particular was worried about something called the "domino theory". Do you remember what the domino theory was? It was a way of thinking that some politicians and citizens in the United States and Europe had. They thought that if one country (like North Korea) could be conquered by the Communists, there other countries would fall one by one, like a series of dominos stacked up in a line. To prevent that, the Americans and their allies felt that North Korea needed to be contained and prevented from taking over South Korea. We also saw how both the U.S.S.R. and China supported the North Koreans, either by sending troops, weapons, money, or advisors.

After that, we learned more about the Korean War itself. Like we saw in the picture at the beginning of this handbook, there were some truly sad moments during the war, like when soldiers lost their friends on the battlefields. The Korean War also saw a lot of civilians get killed in huge massacres. Do you remember who was responsible for many of the deaths? That's right: many of the deaths were Koreans killing Koreans, sometimes people from their own country (like when the bridge was blown up, and many innocent refugees were killed). We saw how the fighting was fierce, but how by the end of the war, everyone was back to where they started from.

The following section showed us what it was like to be a kid living during the Korean War. We used our imaginations to see what it was like to be a kid in the U.S. during the war, and what kinds of things they would have seen and heard about. Do you remember what we saw? We saw that a lot of kids probably wouldn't have understood much about the war because no one actually talked about it. The troops weren't treated like heroes like the veterans of World War Two. We also saw what it would have been like to be a kid living in Korea during the war. As you can probably imagine, it would have been a lot scarier in Korea because of all the fighting and the violence towards innocent civilians.

Next, we saw how the Korean War finally ended. Although the fighting was pretty fierce and tough in the beginning, and although the armies moved around a lot, by the end of the war, things had settled down and everyone wanted the fighting to end. Even so, we saw that it took almost two years for the governments on each side to finally sign the documents to end the fighting. Do you remember what the conditions were that kept the armistice from being signed for so long? The most difficult question was what to do with the prisoners of war. It was finally decided to send everyone back home, and most ended up doing just that.

The final section showed us what the two Koreas (North and South) look like today. We saw that North Korea is still Communist and that they still believe in uniting the two countries under one government. Although the people are poor and don't always have enough to eat, the people are intensely loyal to their leader and to their government. In the South, the economy is doing very well, and life is not much different from the United States. Just about everyone has their own house and a high standard of living. The countries still have skirmishes, and some wonder if there will be another war in the future. We will have to wait and see what happens.

Have you enjoyed learning about Korea from this handbook? It was been an interesting lesson, although it had its sad parts. But why should you care so much about the Korean War? Although some people think that this war was not too prominent, what do you think: should we look at it like that? Not at all. We should always remember how much the soldiers sacrificed to help the Korean people, and how important it was to stop the North Koreans. While not everything about the "domino theory" was 100% accurate, it is always important that people be allowed to choose for themselves what kind of government they want to live under. No one should ever be forced to obey laws and rules that they don't agree with. It was wrong for the North Koreans to try to force their fellow Koreans to think like they did, and the American soldiers fought to stop it from happening.

Although it ended almost sixty years ago, the legend of the Korean War should never be forgotten. Helping out someone else, being willing to die for them, is the most beautiful thing that one human can do for another.

The first state-sponsored memorial (in Washington state) to those who died in the Korean War.[32]

[32] Image source: http://www.ga.wa.gov/visitor/korean/koreanwar.htm

Made in the USA
Middletown, DE
01 March 2016